IMAGES
of America

OAKDALE COTTON MILLS

DOCUMENTING HISTORY. George Reasner, videographer for *Oakdale Cotton Mills: Close-Knit Neighbors*, films Oakdale's historic marker that cites its standing as the oldest continuously operating textile mill in the country. (Patricia M. Koehler.)

ON THE COVER: Employees of Oakdale Cotton Mills assembled in front of their mill building about 1900 for this photograph. The mill began spinning cotton in June 1865. It provided better than average working conditions for employees. A mill village, complete with church, school, store, and barbershop, helped develop a strong sense of community among the workers and a genuine feeling of loyalty to Oakdale. (Oakdale Cotton Mills.)

IMAGES
of America

OAKDALE COTTON MILLS

Mary A. Browning and Patricia M. Koehler

ARCADIA
PUBLISHING

ISBN 978-0-7385-6753-2

Published by Arcadia Publishing
Charleston SC, Chicago IL, Portsmouth NH, San Francisco CA

Printed in the United States of America

Library of Congress Control Number: 2008943249

For all general information contact Arcadia Publishing at:
Telephone 843-853-2070
Fax 843-853-0044
E-mail sales@arcadiapublishing.com
For customer service and orders:
Toll-Free 1-888-313-2665

Visit us on the Internet at www.arcadiapublishing.com

This book is dedicated to those at Oakdale who lived the cotton mill experience during the past 144 years.

Contents

ACKNOWLEDGMENTS

Many individuals and institutions loaned images or provided assistance, for which we are very grateful. They made this book possible. The interest and enthusiasm they and others have shown has been an inspiration.

Topping the list is Oakdale Cotton Mills, which gave every kind of assistance in its power. Billy Ragsdale, president, and Phil Clodfelter, plant manager, have answered our endless questions with patience and grace. Oakdale shared scores of photographs and many of its old records, including employment and store ledgers, dye recipe books, and work diaries kept by various employees over the many years. Photographs not otherwise identified have been loaned from the mill.

Also extremely important to this effort has been the Ragsdale Collection now in the Jamestown Alumni Archives. It consists of business and personal letters and other documents that belonged to William G. Ragsdale Sr. and has opened a priceless window on the early 20th century. The papers were given to the archives by Margaret H. Ragsdale and John R. Ragsdale. Items used from that collection are identified RC.

The Historic Jamestown Society at Mendenhall Plantation provided access to scores of photographs collected as part of the Oakdale Mills Project that it sponsored, and those images are referred to with the acronym HJS.

The Jamestown Library, High Point Library North Carolina Collection, Greensboro Library, Friends Historical Collection at Guilford College, High Point Museum, and Greensboro Historical Museum yielded images and thousands of bits of miscellaneous information.

Individuals who shared memories, photographs, and mementos are Frederick P. Browning, Jean Hill Berghuis, Susan Bullock, Bobby Campbell, Helen Chambers, Margie Cruthis Coleman, Emily Cone, Norma Cruthis, Patricia Vick Cruthis, Tony Cruthis, Norma Dennis, Gordon Dillon, Audrey Garrett Dowdy, Nancy Fortney, Patricia Hatfield, Jackie Hedstrom, Addline Davis Hill, Delbert Hill, Mary Ann Hodgin, Quentin Hodgin, Linda Kenner, Olene Swaim Mabe, Kathleen Mills, Barbara Morgan, Dot Perdue, Coy Proctor, Emily B. Ragsdale, John R. Ragsdale, Paul Rice, Evie Swaim, Allison Wood, Harold Young, Jimmy Young, and Jon Zachman.

We made extensive use of *Jamestown News*, *Greensboro News and Record*, and *High Point Enterprise* articles, also used a photograph from Fairchild Aerial Surveys, and had assistance from Sechrist Funeral Home.

If we have forgotten anyone, please forgive us and remember that your contribution will live on in the pages of this book.

INTRODUCTION

The saga of the southern textile industry is drawing to a close. Billy Ragsdale, president of Oakdale Cotton Mills, described the textile history as one that started in England, went to New England, then to the South, and finally to China. Left behind across the South are abandoned cotton mill buildings waiting for the bulldozer's claws or to be gutted and transformed into offices, shops, or apartments. Houses in the mill villages, once reserved exclusively for mill employees, have been sold off to strangers, seldom to employees, since they could not afford the relatively low cost. But the cohesiveness that once characterized village life as "like a family" cannot be duplicated. Now it resides in the memories of those who lived it.

For one mill, the story is just ending. Oakdale Cotton Mills sits on the edge of Deep River in Jamestown, in a secluded hollow referred to affectionately by its former residents as "Happy Holler."

Its history is unique in several respects. Five generations of the Ragsdale family have shepherded the business and its employees through good times and tough ones over the past 144 years. The ethic that shaped the owners' commitment to employees can be traced in part to the influence of their Quaker roots. The genuine interest in employees ranged from keeping employee numbers at a level that saved jobs but was not cost-effective, to encouraging and providing financial assistance for continued education, to loaning money to buy a home and taking payments out of paychecks. No-interest loans helped tide workers over rough spots, and informal conversations about personal problems that would be considered counseling today guided workers through unfamiliar issues. The sense that every person is valued has been the hallmark of each generation in this remarkable family, and that has been reflected, not only in interactions on the job but in informal situations in the village and elsewhere.

The industry has been stereotyped as paternalistic, that owners early on knew what was best for the mostly poor and undereducated workers, and owners crafted a way of life for them that was stable, sober, and God-fearing. Workers were expected to attend religious services, to show up for work on time, and to avoid the devil drink. Low pay, company store debt, and long hours kept workers in a sort of bondage, never able to get ahead. Company-sponsored activities such as baseball teams generated a fervor that resulted in a sort of loyalty, but it may have been directed more to the workers on the team than to the company itself. Critics claimed that all was done in the name of keeping workers on the job. Reports from longtime Oakdale employees tell a different story, that the Ragsdale family truly cared about its employees.

Part of that atmosphere can be attributed to the size of the company. Oakdale was a small cotton mill by comparison to most. At its peak, it employed 250 workers. The business has obviously grown since its inception in 1865, and it has experienced several large expansions. However, in 1982, Thomas C. Ragsdale Jr. summed up the attitude about growing the business bigger. He explained that he was satisfied with the size of the operation then. He echoed the sentiments of his ancestors when he noted that it is nice to know all the people that work there, to be on a first-name basis, valuing that personal contact.

Despite the concern for its employees, there were factors that Oakdale and other mills could not control in the early years—heat generated by the machinery, humidity that was vital for the cotton's condition, the lint and dust generated by the spinning process. That was the way the early mills functioned. But as the industry developed, Oakdale was ahead of the pack in taking action to improve conditions by installing air-conditioning and dust control, promoting education for children, and providing retirement benefits and hospitalization, for example. Church attendance was encouraged, and the mills often provided land and funds for the establishment of a church nearby. Critics would say it was in the owners' interest to keep employees on the straight and narrow. The other side of the coin is that the owners understood from their own spiritual lives the peace and comfort religion brought. For workers who lived a frugal life, with no great opportunities for improvement in sight and families to raise, religion could be a positive influence and offer hope.

The story of the aftermath of the Civil War in the ravaged South spells out the difficulties of starting over, with bartering as a way of life and ingenuity a necessity for getting business underway. Chapter one explores the history of the area and the metamorphosis of the business from its beginnings with secondhand machinery and little else. The diary of Thomas Cook, the first superintendent, chronicles the frustrations and small victories that marked his first days on the job in 1865 and the gradual growth of the mill. The first member of the Ragsdale family, Joseph Sinclair Ragsdale, joined the business about 1880 and set into motion the dynasty that would govern the mill for five generations. The Ragsdale men also concerned themselves with the growth and condition of the town and were all very active in local government.

Chapter two documents the growth of the mill, from its humble beginning as a small spinning mill, to the addition of dyeing and bleaching of its spun cotton, to its expansion to produce more complex products that required different machinery. However, Oakdale could not stand outside the forces of change, and the impact of overseas competition brought new challenges to keep the business afloat.

Village life, as Oakdale workers describe it, was happy, busy, simple, and caring. Residents were there for one another in the many ways good neighbors are. Some of their stories are included in chapter three, some in the film *Oakdale Cotton Mills: Close-Knit Neighbors*, and others will be archived at Historic Jamestown Society so the story of the vigorous life that existed across the railroad tracks on the edge of town will not be lost.

After the hard work was done, workers, adults and children alike, still had energy to play. Their recreation was simple, given their circumstances. But some former villagers wax nostalgic about the value of that simple time and wish their own children and grandchildren could experience it. Chapter four gives a flavor for their recreation, celebrations, and the mill's outreach to its employees and the community.

The memories will live on, but the life of the mill has finally succumbed to the pressures of a troubled industry and economic era. Oakdale Cotton Mills closed at the end of July 2009 in its 144th year.

One

FOUNDATIONS

The original Jamestown settlement grew up around a gristmill built about 1760 on one of the headwater branches of Deep River by a Pennsylvania Quaker named James Mendenhall. His was only one of the many small manufactories that would be built within a few miles, all making good use of the water power supplied by the river and its creeks—Bull Run Creek among them. These cottage industries used the river to fill and sluice tanyard vats, to mill grain or saw lumber, to turn lathes for wood, or to mill metal parts for the well-known Jamestown rifles. James Mendenhall soon moved on to Georgia but left his son George to run the mills and develop an ambitious plan for a village that was chartered by 1816 and named for his father. Jamestown stood on the high west bank of Deep River. By 1849, it had about 150 inhabitants. It never gained the prominence of Greensboro, the county seat. However, it lay along the Salisbury Stage Road, which connected it to Hillsboro and points north and to Salisbury and points south. It always had a post office, a school, and a substantial prominence as a center of Quaker influence. Deep River Friends Meeting, located a few miles north, was an important Quaker connection. When the North Carolina Railroad laid tracks that roughly paralleled the stage road, the point near the town where the two came closest together pulled the local center of activity away from the old village and toward what became known as Jamestown Depot, or New Jamestown. The first railroad service was in 1852. Near the depot, another road led southeast past another old mill site about a mile away, where Bull Run Creek enters Deep River. Here the Oakdale Cotton Mills story begins.

Cyrus P. Mendenhall (1817–1884). One of James Mendenhall's great-grandsons, Cyrus was instrumental in establishing what would become Oakdale Cotton Mills. Though he grew up in Jamestown, his career was in Greensboro, where he was a lawyer, banker, businessman, mayor, and North Carolina Railroad executive. He joined forces with Ezekiel P. Jones and Grafton Gardner to purchase used cotton spinning equipment from Scott's Factory in Smithfield, Virginia, in 1861, but the Civil War intervened, and the firm of Mendenhall, Jones, and Gardner stored the equipment and instead secured a contract with the Confederate government to manufacture rifles for the Confederate army. They began in Cedar Creek Foundry and Machine Shop, but within a few months, the partners bought an old gristmill located about a mile south of Jamestown. (North Carolina Friends Historical Collection, Guilford College.)

The Old Mill Building. Here Mendenhall, Jones, and Gardner made rifles based upon the U.S. Model 1841 "Mississippi" rifle for the Confederates, using local expertise to produce at least 2,000. This structure escaped destruction by Union army raiders in early 1865 when they were misdirected to a woolen uniform factory in Jamestown. It and a railroad bridge were burned instead.

Henry Potter (1829–1895). Henry and his brother Isaac had owned the building. It stood where Oakdale now stands. It was Logan Factory until a new charter renamed it Oakdale Manufacturing Company in 1873. Cyrus Mendenhall remained a major shareholder until his 1884 death. Potter later worked as the railroad's agent at Jamestown Depot. (HJS.)

Gun Making on Deep River. This display at the Greensboro Historical Museum features five rifles by Mendenhall, Jones, and Gardner and two by Jamestown gun maker H. C. Lamb. The exhibit is part of the John M. and Isabelle Murphy Collection of Confederate Firearms. All Jamestown rifles are highly prized by collectors. (Greensboro Historical Museum; photograph by Jon Zachman.)

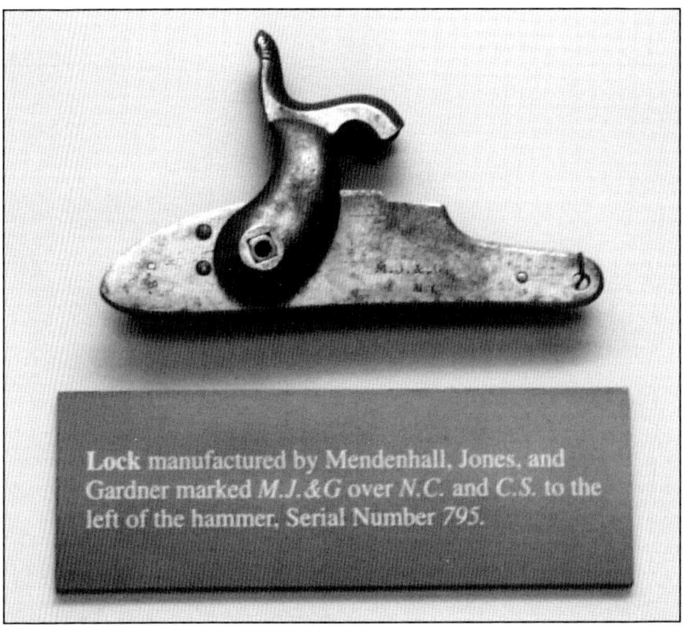

Gun Lock Marked MJG. This gun lock in the display at left is stamped MJ&G. During the Civil War, the Confederate government also established the Florence Armory just north of Jamestown. It took further advantage of local expertise to convert locally made sporting guns to military use and used parts from defunct manufacturers to make new guns for the Confederate army. (Greensboro Historical Museum; photograph by Jon Zachman.)

Thomas H. Cook (1813–1889). The used machinery came by wagon from Danville, Virginia, to the old wooden building where Cook, a 50-year-old former Confederate officer, oversaw its installation. Within the year, Mary Cook and the couple's six children moved from Smithfield, Virginia, to settle permanently in Jamestown. Machinist Jesse Johnson also made that trip and, like Cook, became a permanent transplant to the town.

Thomas Cook's Diary. "I left home for Jamestown, N.C. June 21st, 1865 and arrived at Logan Factory Sunday June 25th 1865. Commenced business on Monday morning June 26th, 1865." So Cook wrote in his pocket diary as he began his 23 years as superintendent of the mill. The diary tells of the first days there, when the water was too low to run the machinery, when it was too high, how much he paid for cotton, when he wrote to his wife, and where he attended worship services. (Patricia M. Koehler.)

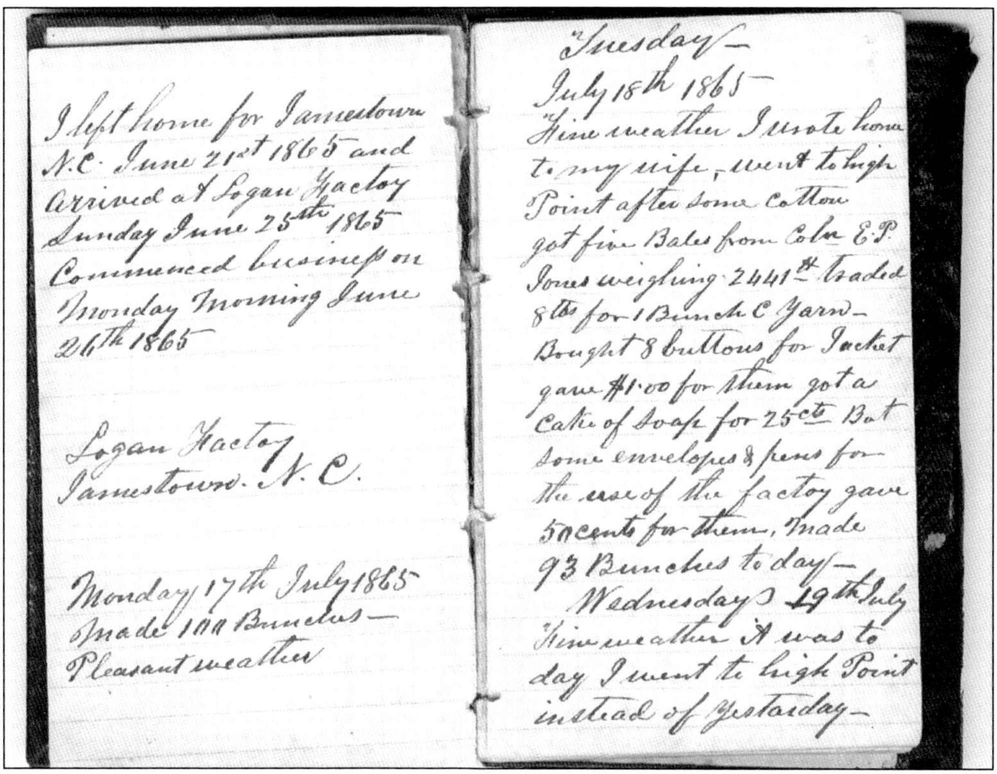
I left home for Jamestown
N.C. June 21st 1865 and
arrived at Logan Factory
Sunday June 25th 1865
Commenced business on
Monday Morning June
26th 1865

Logan Factory
Jamestown. N.C.

Monday 17th July 1865
Made 100 Bunches—
Pleasant weather

Tuesday—
July 18th 1865—
Fine weather I wrote home
to my wife, went to high
Point after some Cotton
got five Bales from Coln E.P.
Jones weighing 2441 lb traded
8 lbs for 1 Bunch C Yarn—
Bought 8 buttons for Jacket
gave \$1.00 for them got a
Cake of Soap for 25cts Bot
some envelopes & pens for
the use of the factory gave
50 cents for them, made
93 Bunches to day—
Wednesday 19th July
Fine weather It was to
day I went to high Point
instead of yesterday—

JOSEPH SINCLAIR RAGSDALE (1836–1903). Ragsdale (left) was also a former Confederate officer, a member of Company F, 54th North Carolina Infantry Regiment, and a graduate of Trinity College. He bought Flint Hill Academy near Jamestown Depot in 1862, and when he returned from the war, he operated the school for two years. He married Emily Jane Idol in 1866. They had four children.

RAGSDALE SET THE PATTERN. About 1880, Ragsdale was hired to look after the business and financial affairs at Oakdale Manufacturing Company. He then headed a group that purchased and incorporated the mill in 1896. As president, he set the mold for mill administration and for civic responsibility, serving as unofficial mayor of the unincorporated community. This leadership role has been followed by his descendants.

William Gannaway Ragsdale (1874–1929). "Will" (right) was Joseph's son. He attended public schools and Guilford College and went to work at Oakdale Cotton Mills in 1892. He was secretary of the corporation by 1900, added the duties of superintendent in 1901, and those of treasurer in 1903 at the death of his father. In 1914, he was elected president and treasurer of Oakdale.

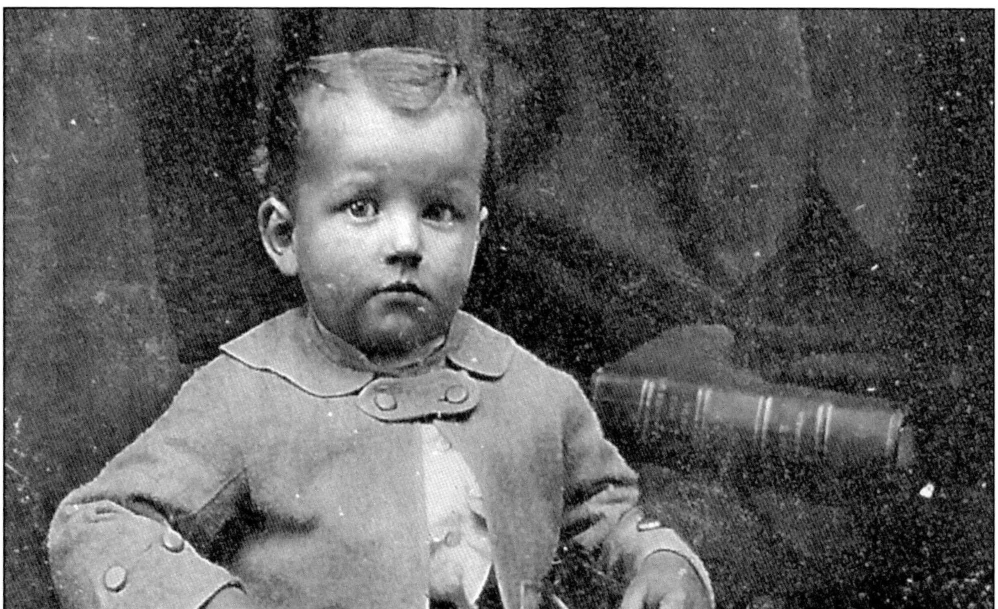

Tintype of Will, About 1875. In 1902, he married Lucy Cook Coffin. They had seven children. Surviving letters in the Ragsdale Collection show the wide range of his responsibilities and interests—church and school, labor practices and politics, family matters, and Oakdale. In declining health from tuberculosis in his last years, he depended upon Oscar M. Bundy to manage the mill during his lengthy absences. (Emily B. Ragsdale.)

Will Ragsdale in His Home Workshop. "This is a photograph of my grandfather, William G. Ragsdale, in the shop/garage at his home taken in the 1920s," says John Ragsdale. "It is the brick building still standing on the property close to the Methodist church. The open bay door is on the right of the picture and faces Main Street. . . . He did have a printing press which was later moved to the mill." The overhead belt and pulley arrangement supplied power. (Emily B. Ragsdale.)

Oscar Mayfield Bundy (1878–1944). Bundy never became president but began as a 12-year-old reeler and advanced to secretary, treasurer, and general manager in 1929 when W. G. Ragsdale Sr. died. In all but title, he filled the temporary top position and was active in local educational, political, and religious affairs. His wife, Nettie Johnson, was a granddaughter of Jesse Johnson, the original Oakdale machinist from Virginia.

William Gannaway Ragsdale Jr. (1911–1969) "Bill" (right) was next in succession at Oakdale. He began work there in 1931 and became president in 1942. He was a Guilford County commissioner for 20 years. He saved many historic properties in and around Jamestown, purchasing them as they became available. He married Mary Elizabeth Lovelace. Their two children are Mary Perry and William G. III. He is shown here with "Clete" Campbell, longtime superintendent at the mill.

Thomas Coffin Ragsdale (1917–1989). "Tom," younger son of W. G. Sr., held a textile management degree and joined Oakdale in 1938, becoming treasurer and then president in 1971. He is well remembered for his role in getting Jamestown chartered as a municipality in 1947 and serving as mayor for many years. He married Margaret Hill in 1942. They had two children: Thomas C. Jr. and John R. (Emily B. Ragsdale.)

THOMAS COFFIN RAGSDALE JR. (1946–1998). "Tommy" represented the fourth generation of Ragsdales at Oakdale. After education and military service, he joined the firm in the early 1970s and served as vice president until taking over as chief executive officer until 1991. He was a teacher at Canterbury School, was active in a variety of civil organizations, and was Jamestown's mayor at the time of his death. He married Emily Dozier Borden in 1980. They had two children. (Emily Ragsdale.)

WILLIAM GANNAWAY RAGSDALE III (BORN 1943). "Billy," son of W. G. Jr., learned the ropes at Oakdale after fulfilling school and service obligations, then struck off on his own when his father died in 1969 and spent 10 years working elsewhere in the textile industry. He returned to Oakdale in 1985 and kept the mill running as long as there was enough business to pay the bills. Following tradition, he served for several years as Jamestown's mayor. He married Katherine Antoniadis. Billy has three children.

Magnolia Farm Centennial Favor, 1966. This drawing was presented to guests at the centennial celebration of Magnolia Farm, a Jamestown landmark. The modest 1866 six-room home built by Joseph and Emily Ragsdale on land purchased from W. G. Sapp, using a small inheritance of Emily's, blossomed into a substantial and comfortable showplace. Its current resident represents the fifth generation of Ragsdales to live here. Early residents walked to the mill from this house. The grounds also hold a handsome barn, numerous outbuildings, and horses grazing in the pasture. The home was just across the Salisbury Stage Road from Flint Hill School, and other Ragsdale family homes are nearby. A residential and business community known as New Jamestown or Jamestown Depot developed near the farm, the school, and the North Carolina Railroad depot, beginning in the 1850s. (High Point Public Library North Carolina Collection.)

Jamestown's Depot. John Ragsdale says that W. G. Ragsdale Sr. first learned of his father's death in 1903 when he called at the depot on his way home from work and found that Joseph's body had been shipped here in a wooden crate from the Charlotte hospital where he had died earlier in the day. Postal Telegraph magnate Clarence H. Mackay often came in his personal railroad car to visit his hunting lodge north of town, leaving the car parked on the siding near the depot during his visit. (HJS.)

Common Sight at the Depot. Over many years, Oakdale's trucks and wagons were familiar sights at the depot, hauling coal, raw materials, and finished product, as this advertising postcard for Acme Trucks proclaims. The early railroad and telegraph were essential to the mill. W. G. Ragsdale Sr. complained to railroad officials in 1909 that "the freight warehouse is entirely too small and . . . passenger accommodations . . . are simply fearful, one little room about 10 x 10 feet for both whites and blacks." (RC.)

WHARTON'S STORE. Henry Clay Briggs said the store was located "over the hill, south of the depot" and that James W. Wharton operated the McConnell Store until he "went off to the Civil War." Store clerk Wharton was in the 1870 census, but Cook's diary reports D. W. C. Benbow was the owner in 1871 and sent Wharton to manage his Greensboro store, while Henry Potter replaced him in the Jamestown establishment. (HJS.)

Post Office, c. 1900. In 1811, Jamestown's first post office was west of Deep River in the old village, but this turn-of-the-century building stood at present 116 East Main Street. Handwriting on the back identifies the following: "Nathan M. Bales and L. L. Hendrix in the doorway, and (left to right) Ethel Daniels, Unknown, Mrs. Carl Bundy (Blanche Williams), Mrs. Shamburger, Erma Bundy, Gertrude Bundy—girl in front, Thelma Lowe, Beulah Dean—third row, Bessie Bevin ?, Mrs. Dan Moore, Mrs. Moore (teacher), Hendrix boy."

Two

THE MILL

The early development of Oakdale Cotton Mills can be followed from June 21, 1865, to January 5, 1875, by reading Supt. Thomas Cook's diary. His first entry, detailing his arrival at the factory, and the photograph of the original frame building, appear in chapter one. The original machinery, in storage in Virginia during the Civil War, was secondhand and proved to be a source of constant breakdowns and resulting work stoppages. Understandably, most of Cook's diary entries focus on weather, the water level of Deep River, the breakdowns and repairs of machinery, difficulty locating cotton to spin, and quantities of yarn produced. Some entries are related to family, church, friends, workers, and business associates.

Initially, the mill was equipped only for carding and spinning. New machinery was installed in January and May 1871—speeders and slubbers from Manchester, England, and drawing and spinning frames. Cook recorded that, despite the downtime for installing new flooring and machinery, comparing earnings for 1871 with those of 1870, "Our numbers average much finer." In March 1872, the foundation for a picker room was dug. Other sources document the evolution of the mill after 1875, revealing ongoing upgrades to the machinery and additions to the buildings that over time created a modern, computerized spinning and dyeing operation.

Over time, the product line included twine and cordage for construction trades and bundling in such businesses as publishing, laundries, bakeries, agriculture, and fishing. Noting the emergence of types of tape that could replace twine, Oakdale expanded their product line to include plied yarns for weavers and knitters. Employees ranged in number from 70 in 1870 to a high of 250 in the 1930s through the 1950s, when the mill operated three shifts. A gradual decline began in the 1970s from about 174 employees to only 50 in 2005. The continuing decline in numbers of employees is directly related to overseas competition. With 18 employees in 2009, Oakdale Cotton Mills sought niche product opportunities to maintain a viable business in its 144th year.

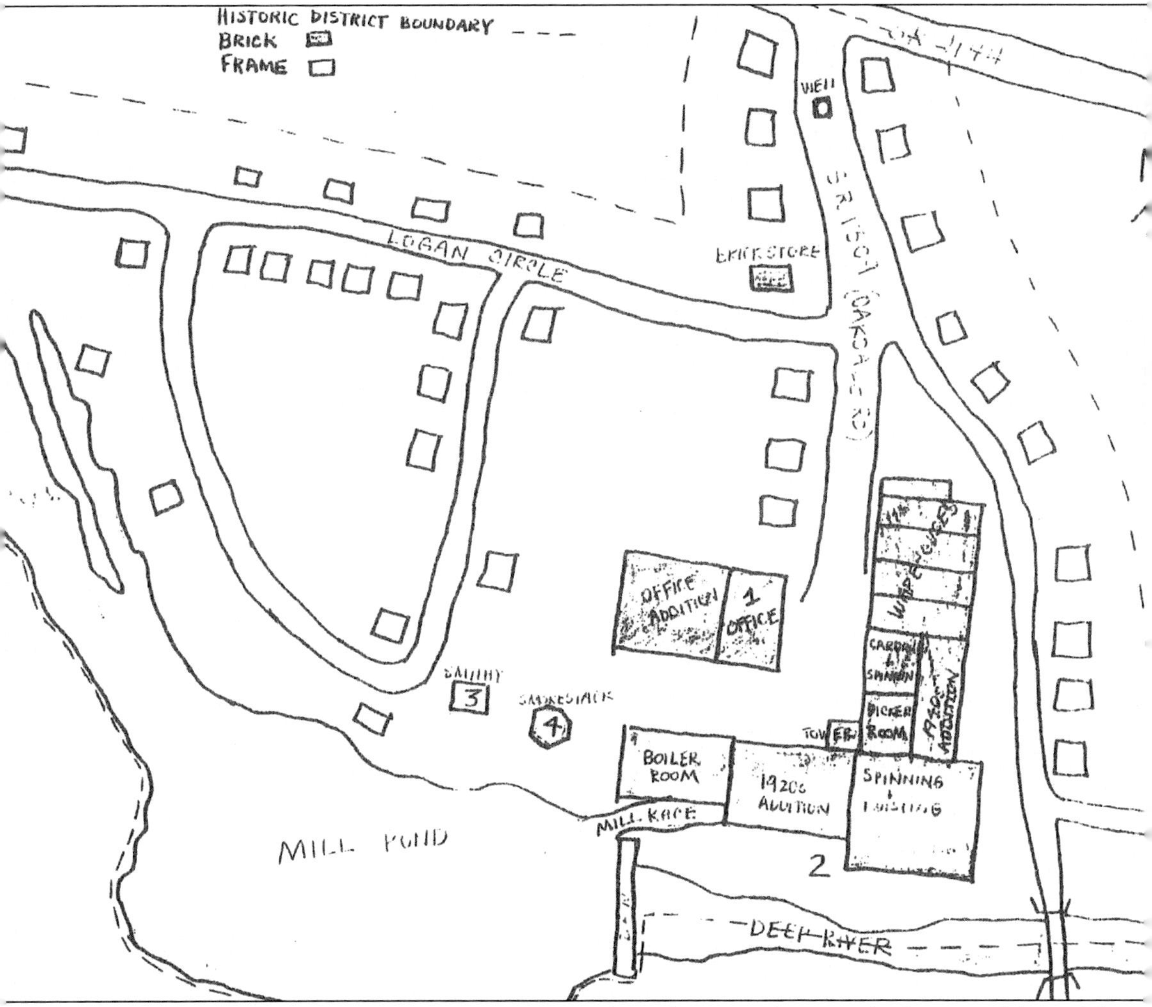

Oakdale's Mill Pond, Millrace, and Dam. These elements, shown at the bottom of this 1975 sketch, have not moved since 1865, when the factory works depended entirely upon the river and the wheel to drive the machinery of the mill. In 1870, the vertical wheel was generating only 40 horsepower, but that drove 2,400 spindles. The state of the wheel itself was a constant concern, as were the conditions of the dam and the millrace that diverted and controlled the flow of the river to the wheel. Thomas Cook's diaries repeatedly note in the 1870s that the "Factory stopped" while brief or lengthy repairs or improvements were made. Substantial work was done on the millrace in 1875 to ensure that stones from the mill's foundation would not loosen and fall on the wheel.

Getting a Makeover. The original wooden building was replaced around 1889, using bricks made on-site. John Henry Hodgin, water boy for the brick masons, explained years later that half of the old three-story frame mill was torn down, making room for the new building. When the first half of the brick building was completed, machinery was transferred and the remaining frame portion torn down, allowing the brick structure to be completed.

New Stone Dam Replaced the Old One, 1901. The wooden dam was 20 feet high and 260 feet long. It collected water and diverted it through a 250-foot millrace. Not long after the new stone dam was completed, high water washed the top away, along with the bridge just downstream. Workmen can be seen in this photograph standing on the riverbed.

At the Waterwheel Intake and Retaining Wall. George L. Hodgin (1868–1947), longtime engineer at the mill, kept a diary from 1895 to 1944, which naturally paid attention to his own concerns and preserved a good record of structural and mechanical work at the mill. In the winter of 1898–1899, he noted that the old waterwheel was torn out and new ones (44-foot Leffel special dual-turbine wheels) were installed. It increased horsepower to 190—if the water supply was adequate. The bridge over Deep River can be seen on the right. One bridge was washed away in August 1908 and replaced that September. A new steel bridge was built in April 1922, so this photograph was probably taken after that time.

Bob McGhee and George Hodgin. George L. Hodgin's diary notes that on his watch, many additional changes were made to the power supply. In October 1913, a new brick boiler room was started, and two new boilers replaced three old ones. In 1915, another new boiler went in and a new 100-horsepower Hamilton Corliss engine. In 1922, it was out with the vertical S. Morgan Smith waterwheel and in with the new horizontal wheel, which was first run on December 20. In 1937, the changeover to electricity was completed, and the steam engine was used only to power the dye house. The retired bronze wheel now rests quietly on the riverbed, relic of another time and too cumbersome to move. The beautiful brass steam whistle, another relic, can be seen under a lamp shade in the mill office lobby.

Steam Powers the Mill. When Robert McGehee (McGhee) began work at Oakdale, he said the mill was powered by a huge steam engine, fed from three boilers. The steam line from the boiler is at the top of the picture. The condenser is on the right and the shielded drive train on the left. Robert Lee Garrett was mill engineer in the early 1900s when this picture was taken. (Audrey Garrett Dowdy.)

Moving Forward. By 1889, new carding, spinning, and twisting sections were operating in the expanded mill. Carding machines, which continue to clean the cotton, are on the left behind the drawing frames. Drawing frames straighten fibers, which are compressed into a continuous flat bat of cotton by lap winders (front right). Lint flies from the machines and collects on workers' clothing, eyebrows, and hair, thus the demeaning nickname "lintheads."

NOISE, NOISE. Belts, wheels, and pulleys powered by the waterwheel ran the noisy machines. Cook wrote in January 1871, "Had to lengthen the shaft to make it run the whole length of the frame, as I did not want the two belt pulleys to run so close together at the alley. It might catch the girls' frocks." Women wore their hair pinned up because of a similar concern.

OAKDALE RING TWISTING FRAMES, C. 1890. Several threads are twisted together to increase size and strength and are wound on a bobbin for further processing, depending on the type of product to be manufactured. Cotton fiber requires a certain level of humidity so it does not become brittle. The early spinning and twister rooms were hot and humid.

LONG HOURS, HARD WORK. In the early days, there was one shift from 6:00 a.m. to 6:00 p.m., and some part of that day was lit by oil lamps and heated by woodstoves in the winter. Oakdale added a 12-hour night shift in 1895. Eventually 12-hour shifts gave way to eight hours, running from 6:00 a.m. to 2:00 p.m. and 2:00 p.m. to 10:00 p.m. In 1947, Oakdale started a third shift,

and the mill worked around the clock again. Boys, girls, and some women worked in bare feet, and the wood floors between the rows of spinning frames were rough from the doffing carts that rolled up and down. Feet were dirty and splinters common. Douglas Carter confessed that he was ashamed of his dirty feet when a lady came into the mill to see the new print machine.

Simpler Times. Ball winding machines are in the background and hanks of yarn in the foreground. At the time of this photograph, yarn was dyed in hanks and could then be run off into balls. (The mill still ran ball winders until it closed recently.) Note the pair of fire buckets hanging from a post on the left. The danger of fire is ever present because of sparks from friction and the flammability of cotton.

The Shipping Department, c. 1890. The bundles at lower left appear to be wrapped and tied for delivery. The stacks on the table may be bunches of yarn, which Thomas Cook referred to in his diary in numbers produced by the end of the day. Cotton on the floor behind the woodstove appears to be bundled in hanks. The shipper's table in the back right is still in the mill.

SOUTH VIEW OF THE MILL. High water in March 1912 rose in the basement level of the mill to 3 feet, 10 inches and washed away 40 cords of wood that were stored to stoke the woodstoves in the mill. But that was not a record. In August 1908, flooding brought water to the highest level since 1865 when it washed out several bridges.

COLOR COMES TO OAKDALE. According to mill records, yarn and twine dyeing began in 1896. The single-story dye house at the edge of the river was built in 1900. Soon after, the DuPont Company paid for young John Henry Hodgin to study chemistry at Guilford College at New Garden. He eventually became supervisor of the dye house, where he spent most of his 42-year career. He lived to be 99.

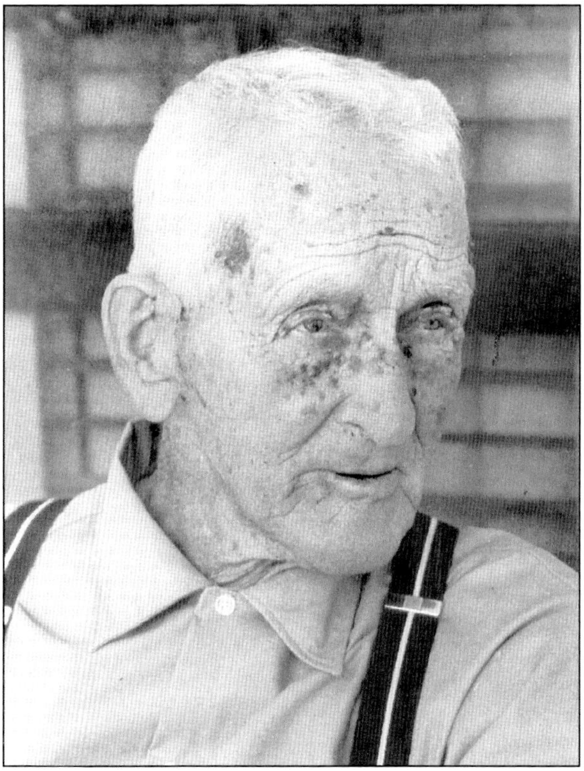

Color Brightens the Day. When the dye process was begun, dyeing was done by hand. After 24 hours of bleaching, 5 pounds of yarn at a time was placed in a tub with dye and turned by hand every five minutes for even coloring. John Henry's granddaughter, Mary Ann Hodgin, remembers that he often displayed his hands and arms when he came home, announcing, "Look what color I am today." (Mary Ann Hodgin.)

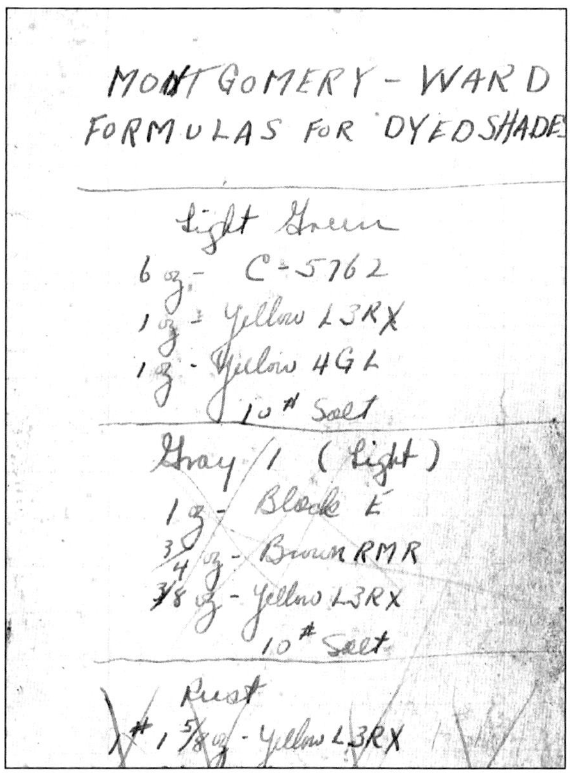

MONTGOMERY-WARD
FORMULAS FOR DYED SHADES

Light Green
6 oz. - C-5762
1 oz - Yellow L3RX
1 oz - Yellow 4GL
10# Salt

Gray /1 (Light)
1 oz - Black E
3/4 oz - Brown RMR
3/8 oz - Yellow L3RX
10# Salt

Rust
1 5/8 oz - Yellow L3RX

Color Formulas. A page from the mill's early dye notebook gives the recipes for a variety of colors. Salt sets the dye. Jean Hill Berghuis remembers her father, James Hill, bringing home dyed threads from the ends of spools. Her mother put them in a bowl with hardboiled eggs, water, and vinegar and made beautiful Easter eggs. But the eggs were for decoration; they were not safe to eat.

Not in a Hurry. With the railroad depot a mile away, raw cotton, as well as everything else for the mill and the store, had to be ordered and brought from the depot to the mill. Finished products were hauled to the depot for shipment. The mill owned three teams of mules and maintained a smithy at the mill. In 1910, Gene Toombs drives one of the mule teams.

Ready to Be Shipped. James Dodson Adams, born in 1885, began working at Oakdale in the shipping department from 6:00 a.m. to 6:00 p.m. for 50¢ a day when he was around 10 years old. He worked at one time in carding and retired after more than 50 years at the mill. Adams was a whistler, and his grandson, Harold Young, said, "You always heard him before you saw him."

Families under Pressure. The number of workers here suggests it dates to before 1901. Young boys were sweepers or doffers, who swept up lint and cotton debris or quickly removed full bobbins from spindles, tossed them in a wheeled cart, and placed empty bobbins on the spindles. Young girls and women were spinners or winders. Men worked with machines getting the cotton ready for spinning. The Federal Child Labor Law went into effect September 1, 1917, and North Carolina

passed a Compulsory Education and Child Labor Law on March 10, 1919. Children between the ages of 8 and 14 were required to attend school regularly when it was in session. Local pressure had been underway earlier. In 1915, employee Kate Smith wrote to Ragsdale about her dire finances, noting that she was "compelled to send 4 to school this year." (RC.)

Part of the Job. James Wood, a mill employee, sits astride a company mule with his son, Howard, who became an employee when he grew up. Gene Toombs grooms another mule in front of the mill office in 1910. Cotton warehouses are in the background. Wood, a carpenter, hauled wood to the mill to make barrel staves for shipping barrels. He also helped care for the mules at the mill barn.

Harvest Means Work, Too. At the sheds behind the office, near the water tower, a pile of corn needs to be shucked, probably to feed the mules over the winter. From left to right, Oscar Bundy, Gene Toombs, unidentified, Josh Wood, Jim Wood, and unidentified attack the task in 1910. The nearby Ragsdale farm may have been where the corn was grown. Some mill employees are known to have threshed wheat and done other farming tasks there.

WORK RULES POSTED. In 1901, William G. Ragsdale assumed the role of mill superintendent. His management style is evident in the work rules that he established. The two weeks' notice rule may have helped stabilize the workforce, some of whom might have responded to efforts of nearby mills to lure them away. Mill owners would plead innocence, but there appeared to be a certain amount of solicitation of workers. (Emily Ragsdale.)

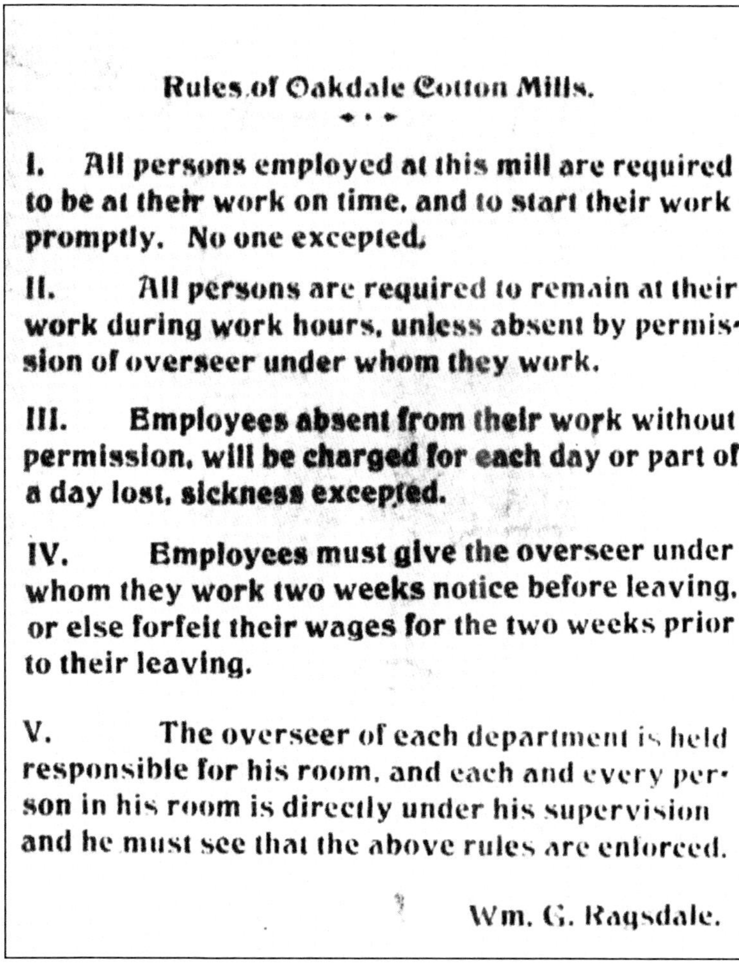

Rules of Oakdale Cotton Mills.

I. All persons employed at this mill are required to be at their work on time, and to start their work promptly. No one excepted.

II. All persons are required to remain at their work during work hours, unless absent by permission of overseer under whom they work.

III. Employees absent from their work without permission, will be charged for each day or part of a day lost, sickness excepted.

IV. Employees must give the overseer under whom they work two weeks notice before leaving, or else forfeit their wages for the two weeks prior to their leaving.

V. The overseer of each department is held responsible for his room, and each and every person in his room is directly under his supervision and he must see that the above rules are enforced.

Wm. G. Ragsdale.

COMING AND GOING. An artist's rendering of Oakdale Cotton Mills dates from about 1913. The image appears to have been used on a letterhead and in advertisements. It read, "Oakdale Cotton Mills, Manufacturers of Cotton Yarns and Twines. Bleachers and Dyers." It also identified F. H. Fries as vice president. The horse-drawn wagons and buggies create a sense of the period.

EASY AS IT LOOKS. In mid-1918, Oakdale management decided to replace its mules and wagons with two Acme trucks. The Acme Company used information from William Ragsdale's testimonial letter to advertise its trucks on postcards, touting the total repair bill for 19 months at 15¢ for both vehicles. The savings amounted to about $2,000 a year, and loading and unloading coal for the boilers became a much easier task.

COAL AND WOOD STOCKPILED. Coal was in short supply after World War I, and regional coal committees regulated its commercial use to 48 hours per week during the winter of 1919. Oakdale Cotton Mills appealed for permission to operate full time, given their use of water power for half of the operation and their foresight to stockpile coal and wood for the mill and the village. Permission was granted. (RC.)

Unions Circulate Handbills. Labor unrest during the late 1880s and early 1900s led to increased interest in unionization. It was thought that Northern business interests promoted this effort to reduce the South's market share. As pressure mounted for greater production for the same wage, the United Textile Workers of America called a general strike for September 1, 1934, hoping to organize large numbers of textile workers. (RC.)

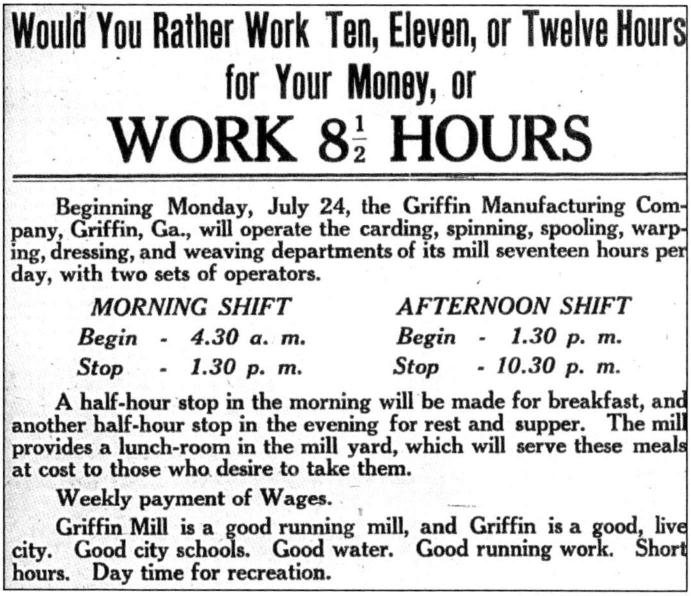

Would You Rather Work Ten, Eleven, or Twelve Hours for Your Money, or

WORK 8½ HOURS

Beginning Monday, July 24, the Griffin Manufacturing Company, Griffin, Ga., will operate the carding, spinning, spooling, warping, dressing, and weaving departments of its mill seventeen hours per day, with two sets of operators.

MORNING SHIFT	AFTERNOON SHIFT
Begin - 4.30 a. m.	Begin - 1.30 p. m.
Stop - 1.30 p. m.	Stop - 10.30 p. m.

A half-hour stop in the morning will be made for breakfast, and another half-hour stop in the evening for rest and supper. The mill provides a lunch-room in the mill yard, which will serve these meals at cost to those who desire to take them.

Weekly payment of Wages.

Griffin Mill is a good running mill, and Griffin is a good, live city. Good city schools. Good water. Good running work. Short hours. Day time for recreation.

Unrest and Trouble. A chain-link fence topped by barbed wire surrounds Oakdale mill, a reminder of the "flying squadrons," union organizers that entered mills to coerce workers to join the strike. When they visited Oakdale and other mills, the owners closed the mills. Billy Ragsdale tells, "There was a little bit of violence, but they left." In 1935, Oakdale completed the fence on the back side of the mill for security.

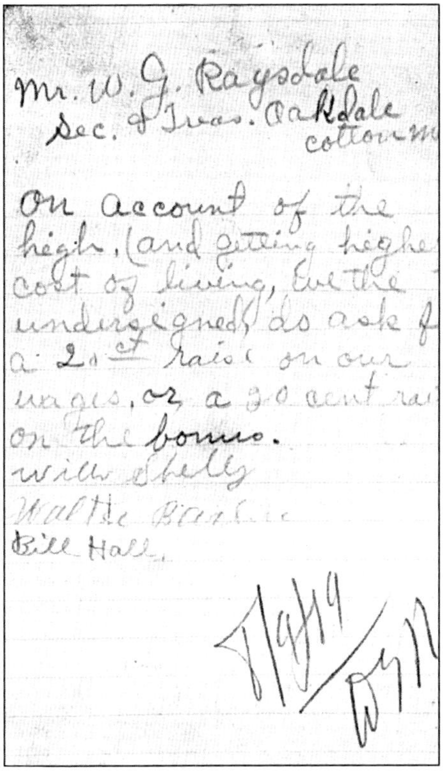

Mr. W. G. Ragsdale
Sec. & Treas. Oakdale
cotton m

On account of the
high, (and getting highe
cost of living, we the
undersigned, do ask f
a 2 ct raise on our
wages, or a 30 cent rai
on the bonus.
Will Shelly
Walter [illegible]
Bill Hall.

TELLING IT LIKE IT IS. Oakdale workers as a whole may have felt no need for a union because of the open-door policy of the owners. Workers could take their concerns directly to the front office. Twenty-nine signatures accompanied this August 1919 request for higher wages. (RC.)

FRIENDS AND EMPLOYEES. From left to right, Buddy Davis, Bob Davis, and Ed Hassell manned the carpenter shop in 1941. William G. Ragsdale, an avid hunter, invited Bob Davis to go bird hunting with him at times. In the early 1920s, Ragsdale asked Davis to circulate petitions, encouraging the school district to lengthen the school year from six to eight months. Ragsdale maintained a genuinely personal relationship with his employees.

GROWING AGAIN. The 1941 expansion enclosed the basement dye house, considered the first floor. The second floor was designated for Brownell twisting machines and the third floor for Abbott winders and twisters. Doubling was done on the third floor.

NOT SO HIGH AND DRY. In the spring of 1941, when work began to expand the dye house building to three stories, the mill pond was drained. The top of the dam is visible on the left, appearing to be level with the tops of the basement windows. The dye house has been flooded a number of times over the years, the levels documented by employees' notations on the wall.

Boilers Need Fed. Bob McGhee, fireman at the front boiler room, works hard to keep three boilers fired up. The mill used coal as power for the dye house until about 1970. McGhee's system was to go across the beds of coals each 15 minutes to keep the fires even. He admitted it took some bit of shoveling to keep the fires hot and the steam up.

Belching Smoke. The giant smokestack's black emission is evidence that the boilers are burning lots of coal. Its impact on the environment and on people must have contributed additionally to breathing problems that some mill workers experienced. Dusty dirt roads and yards, cotton lint and dust, and coal smoke were part of the living conditions that workers accepted for a job and a place to live.

A Good Day Ahead. On the way to work, from left to right, Kathleen Mills, Lillian Hodgin, Agatha Campbell, and Leona Campbell carry their lunches in paper sacks. Kathleen Mills was born in the village and worked at the mill for 47 years, starting in 1944 when the mill recruited her during the war. She worked different jobs in the mill, including managing the cafeteria for eight years until it closed.

Chowing Down. Before the mill opened the cafeteria, workers carried a lunch or a family member, often a child, brought a basket dinner or supper to the worker and visited with them while they ate. Many children learned their parent's job by watching. At one time, Earl Garrett pushed a railroad baggage cart along Oakdale Road, stopping at houses to collect meals for workers.

SECOND SHIFT. The tower housed the stairway to the second and third floors. Margie Cruthis Coleman or her sister Shirley brought their father, Hillery, his supper and met him on the third-floor landing, where they would visit while he ate. The doorway opened into the spinning room and the twister room beyond, where he worked. Sometimes the child would follow him back into the mill and visit with village people she knew.

COOKING ON THE JOB. Some workers solved their meal needs on the job. Harlan Young worked in the boiler room, and when the boilers were fired, he placed an aluminum foil–wrapped potato inside the boiler door. In 10 minutes, he had a perfectly baked potato. He cooked hamburgers in the boiler, also. A can of pork and beans placed on a steam pipe in the morning was boiling hot for lunch. (Billy Ragsdale.)

Anxious to Work. Myrtle Scott, born January 4, 1894, appears in Oakdale's time book in 1906, when she was approximately 12 years old. In an early interview, she said, "I went to work at Oakdale when I was about 10 or 11 years old, but I had run my age up in order to go to work." Her name appears on an employee list for May 1955, at least 49 years later.

Eyeing the Machine. Lena McGee, born September 16, 1890, began work at Oakdale when she was 10. Supt. Stephen Bundy claimed that parents started their children working in the mill at a young age so he could raise them. Adventurous as a child, Lena explored most areas of the mill, except the dynamo room. She even climbed around under the warehouses. Above, Lena is tending the Abbott winder.

Longest Service at Oakdale. Oakdale Cotton Mills had no retirement policy. Lena McGee retired in June 1970, with 70 years of service. Personnel manager Sam Strickland holds a spool of Oakdale thread, a symbol of Lena's years at the mill. Lena remembered that, when she was young, the dark parts of winter working days were lighted by the dynamo and that the light cords would be tied up out of the way in the summer. The doffers would sometimes go for a quick swim below the millrace while waiting for bobbins to be filled again. There were fights between boys and between girls, sometimes over boyfriends. She noted the outstanding efforts made by the mill to improve worker safety over her years of employment. Her fondest memories include the antics of young workers, although she never admitted that she was involved. (Photograph by Jim Wommack.)

He Knew How. Oakdale relied on master mechanic Henry Garrett, shown in October 1974 with an unidentified employee. He started work at the mill when he was 16 and retired at 75. According to Phillip Clodfelter, plant manager, Henry headed up "the shop," which included Lester Breedlove and Harlan Young: "Henry could do just about anything, including plumbing, electrical and machining. He was well respected by everyone I know."

Keeping the Mill Running. Limon Hodgin (left), secretary of Oakdale Cotton Mills, is seen here with Henry Garrett in October 1974. Hodgin was responsible for purchasing raw material, machinery, and parts for the mill. Until machinery became more complex, Garrett could often make a needed part and avoid costly shutdowns. Hodgin and Garrett grew up together and were honored at a reception when they retired at the same time.

Mechanized Now. Gone are the days when bales of cotton were delivered from the depot by mule-drawn wagon. In his diary, Thomas Cook wrote that he bought or traded for loose cotton by the pound locally because cotton was scarce after the Civil War. A bale of cotton weighs about 500 pounds; it would take a while to accumulate a bale of cotton buying by the pound.

The Way It Used to Be. First stop was the opening room, where hoppers tear cotton into tufts so the fibers will be easier to clean and card. To get a good mix of cotton, an operator would pull thin layers of cotton off each bale and load them into the hopper. The bales shown would take about 12 hours to process. After December 2002, Oakdale no longer bought and processed raw cotton. Instead, they bought spun yarn, which eliminated the spinning aspect of the business by the end of 2004.

Getting Ready to Twist. Howard Wood refills the twisting frame, which will twist multiple strands together to produce plied twine. He is standing on the guard rail to reach the top row. When young doffers could not reach the top row on spinner frames, they would climb the frame to remove the full spools.

Commercial Display Rack, c. 1955. Oakdale Cotton Mills spun and dyed a variety of twine and yarn products. The motto on the twine display states, "When It's Bound With Twine, It's Bound to HOLD." The product was promoted for wrapping, handicraft, parcel post, household, garden, fishing, kites, butcher, and mason needs. Yarn customers ranged from weavers and knitters to manufacturers of heavier items such as upholstery fabric.

Progress Underway. Old ring spinning frames are removed in anticipation of the newer, open-end spinning frames. The flooring needed to be replaced or repaired, and other adjustments involved much planning. A downside to the new equipment was that fewer operators would be needed.

New Open-End Spinning Frames. According to Thomas Ragsdale Jr., open-end spinning was introduced around 1972. Oakdale's first such frames were installed in November 1974. The equipment was revolutionary in that it eliminated two steps in the process. New equipment became more automated, and a higher level of skill was needed to run machines. Shown above are, from left to right, Charles McDaniel, Henry Garrett, Clarence Kirkman, and Harlan Young.

Bound for the Depot. Over many years, Oakdale's trucks were familiar sights at the Jamestown Depot. Vernon Clark (left) poses with Charles McDaniel. The Oakdale logo graces every carton. (RC.)

Checking Things Out. Charles McDaniel (front left) and Harlan Young (front right) are backed, from left to right, by Odell Campbell, Henry Garrett, and James Breedlove. McDaniel started at Oakdale as a truck driver in 1961. Pictured here in 1982, he was superintendent and general manager.

The Fix-It Men. In the machine shop are, from left to right, Charlie Harvell, Elwood Campbell, and an unidentified man. Thomas C. Ragsdale Jr. commented in 1982 that the mill made a lot of its own gears and parts, but the machinery was becoming more complex and often needed to be ordered from a company. He regretted that the best machinery was European because he preferred to buy in America.

Changing Shifts. In 1982, Thomas C. Ragsdale Jr. discussed the company's effort to keep three shifts running by cutting back a day per week if necessary rather than close down a shift and let workers go. His attitude reflects that of William G. Ragsdale in 1922, whose policy of "carrying extra help" when he could have pared his costs so frustrated one supervisor that he resigned.

Clearing the Air. Starting in 1970, Oakdale tackled the problem of controlling cotton dust levels in the mill. A pilot project involved Bahnson cleaning equipment, manufactured in nearby Winston-Salem. Dust is drawn into the duct work at the ceiling and carried out of the building. Oakdale continued to monitor dust levels and installed newer, more efficient equipment well before the government mandated dust control.

Pulmonary Function Test. In time, it became clear that cotton mill workers were contracting respiratory illnesses from constant exposure to cotton dust. Brown lung disease (byssinosis) was identified, and in 1978, OSHA set cotton dust standards. Ventilating systems were mandated, and once a year, employees took a breathing test. Above, Thomas Ragsdale Sr., company president, was no exception.

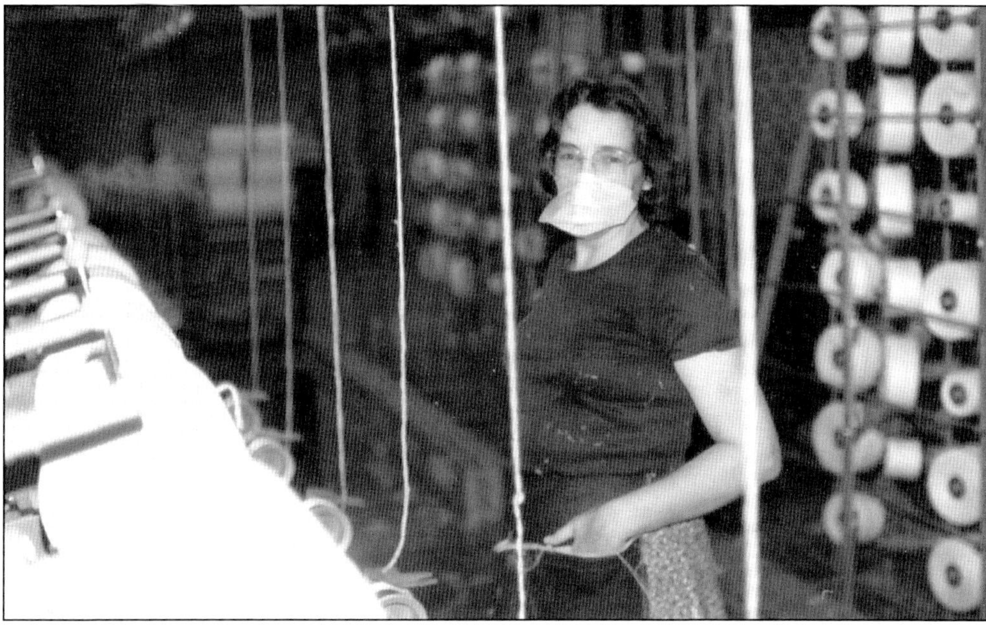

Avoiding Dust. Face masks were available, although they were often rejected because of discomfort. Meeting OSHA standards was costly to the industry, but the incidence of brown lung disease declined. Oakdale Cotton Mills settled three serious cases of brown lung disease. The issue was complicated across the industry because many workers were heavy smokers. This unidentified worker's shirt is dotted with lint.

Noise Abatement. In the early 1980s, efforts began to control noise levels. Sound suppression curtains were installed around machines, and fiber gears replaced metal ones. New equipment must meet noise level requirements. Often one needed to speak loudly into someone's ear to be heard. Juanita Jones tests hearing protection muffs. Although signs advised workers that earplugs must be worn, workers often choose not to because of discomfort.

Progress Continues. The 1941 expansion of the mill was followed by smaller projects over the years to keep the mill efficient and up-to-date. In the 1980s, a second major expansion got underway to make room for new machinery and to expand production. One floor was designated for Volkmann twisters. A warehouse for finished goods found a home in the back, and another area became carton storage.

Volkmann Twisters Expand Production. Volkmann twisters were added between 1970 and 1990; their ability to twist yarn and put it on a cone in one process made them particularly desirable. However, they were designed for small-ply yarn used in knitting and weaving, and ring twisters continued in use because of their efficiency for large-ply twines.

The Price of Progress. Construction for carton storage obscured part of the tower, which is eloquently described in the National Register of Historic Places Inventory-Nomination Form for Oakdale Cotton Mill Village. It states that its Italianate character is most evident in the tower with more ornate brickwork than in the mill's other structures. The mill itself has been described elsewhere as among the most architecturally significant in the state.

Unloading a Monster. A spinning frame, shipped from Canada, waits to be moved into the mill. This spinning frame spins very coarse yarn that would be used for upholstery or household water filters. The yarn is more than twice the thickness of any that Oakdale could spin on existing frames, according to Phillip Clodfelter, plant manager.

DYE HOUSE, 1986. The computerized dye house with its huge vats is a far cry from when John Henry Hodgin's arms and hands displayed the color of the day. Heat and humidity may be the only similarity. Spools are loaded on yarn carriers that sit down in the cylindrical vats and rotate for even coloring. The company matched standard colors but also maintained an extensive color library.

PHILLIP CLODFELTER, PLANT MANAGER. Phil started in a mill while he was still in high school. He has worked many different jobs at Oakdale, so he is a knowledgeable manager. He supervised the million-dollar equipment upgrade in 1995, then in 1997 returned to his former assignment as plant manager. He echoed the sentiment of Pres. Billy Ragsdale that the mill would continue to operate as long as there was business to be had.

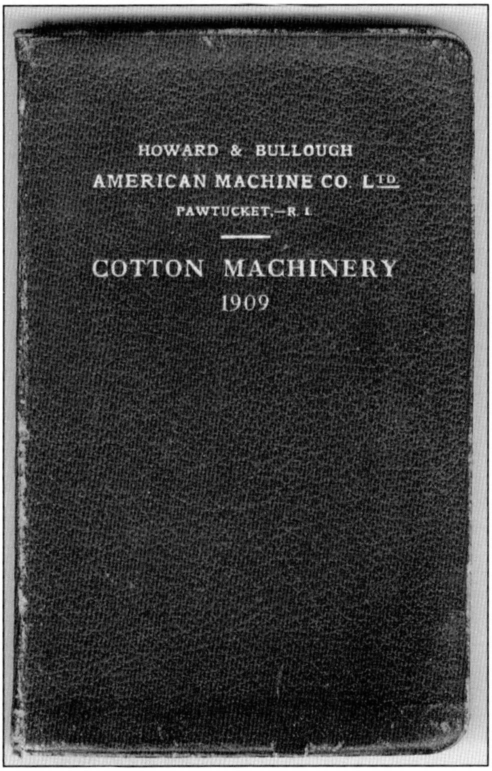

EARLY REFERENCE. Supt. S. L. McClure's signature is found inside this 1909 leather-bound volume, along with a notation that indicates he owned it while working in Virginia. It is an illustrated catalogue of a wide range of cotton machinery built by Howard and Bullough in Pawtucket, Rhode Island. It also contains information about floor space, speeds, productions, gearing diagrams, and useful tables. (Emily Ragsdale.)

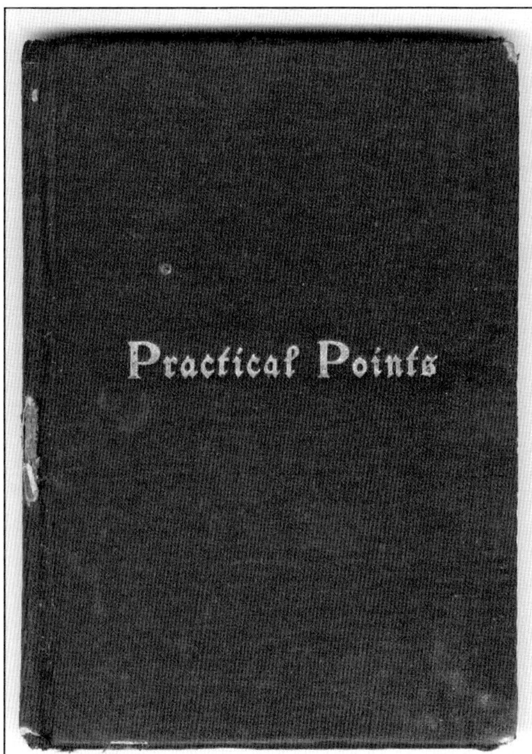

PRACTICAL POINTS. This small volume bears the signature of William G. Ragsdale and the date October 16, 1895. The book is in a question-and-answer format, a study guide intended for engineers, firemen, electricians, motormen, and machinists: "The book treats on boilers, engines, firing, combustion, indicators, dynamos, motors, electricity and has valuable receipts and rules." Those topics were relevant to the daily operation of Oakdale Cotton Mills. (Emily Ragsdale.)

Three

The Village

Cotton mills were often built some distance from towns, and it was common for mill owners to build houses near the mill to attract workers. The location of Oakdale Cotton Mills on the banks of Deep River was quite rural, and Thomas Cook noted in his diary on July 31, 1865, "Most of the hands do not live on the place as there is no houses for them to live in." As a startup mill, the number of hands needed was probably minimal, possibly locals who came on foot, horseback, or by wagon. Cook's diary entry suggests that at least some of the hands did live on the place. So the nucleus of the Oakdale Cotton Mills' village dates roughly to the origin of the mill itself.

As the mill expanded and new mills opened in the more populous towns of nearby Greensboro and High Point, competition for area workers grew. In addition, sharecroppers and small-land farmers became potential workers, but they all needed housing.

The company store ledger, 1868–1894, suggests that some houses existed early in this period. An advertisement for mill hands in 1873 stated that comfortable housing was available. Joseph S. Ragsdale wrote to Rep. Thomas Settle in January 1895 about proposed state legislation to eliminate night work in the mills: "I have hands from Reidsville Cotton Mills and Greensboro Cotton Mills (both broke and stopped) who came and asked for night work. I went to the expense of several thousand dollars to build houses for them to live in and started a night force." He added that the legislation would throw 25 families out of work.

A one-story brick store was built in 1901, and the village continued to develop. In April 1910, in a letter of recommendation for John B. Ridge, the treasurer of the mill wrote, "During 1915 and 1916 we contracted with him to build 8 six-room tenements, a superintendent's house and a Church for our company." The National Register of Historic Places Inventory-Nomination Form for Oakdale Cotton Mills Village reports that 33 houses were built between 1900 and 1924.

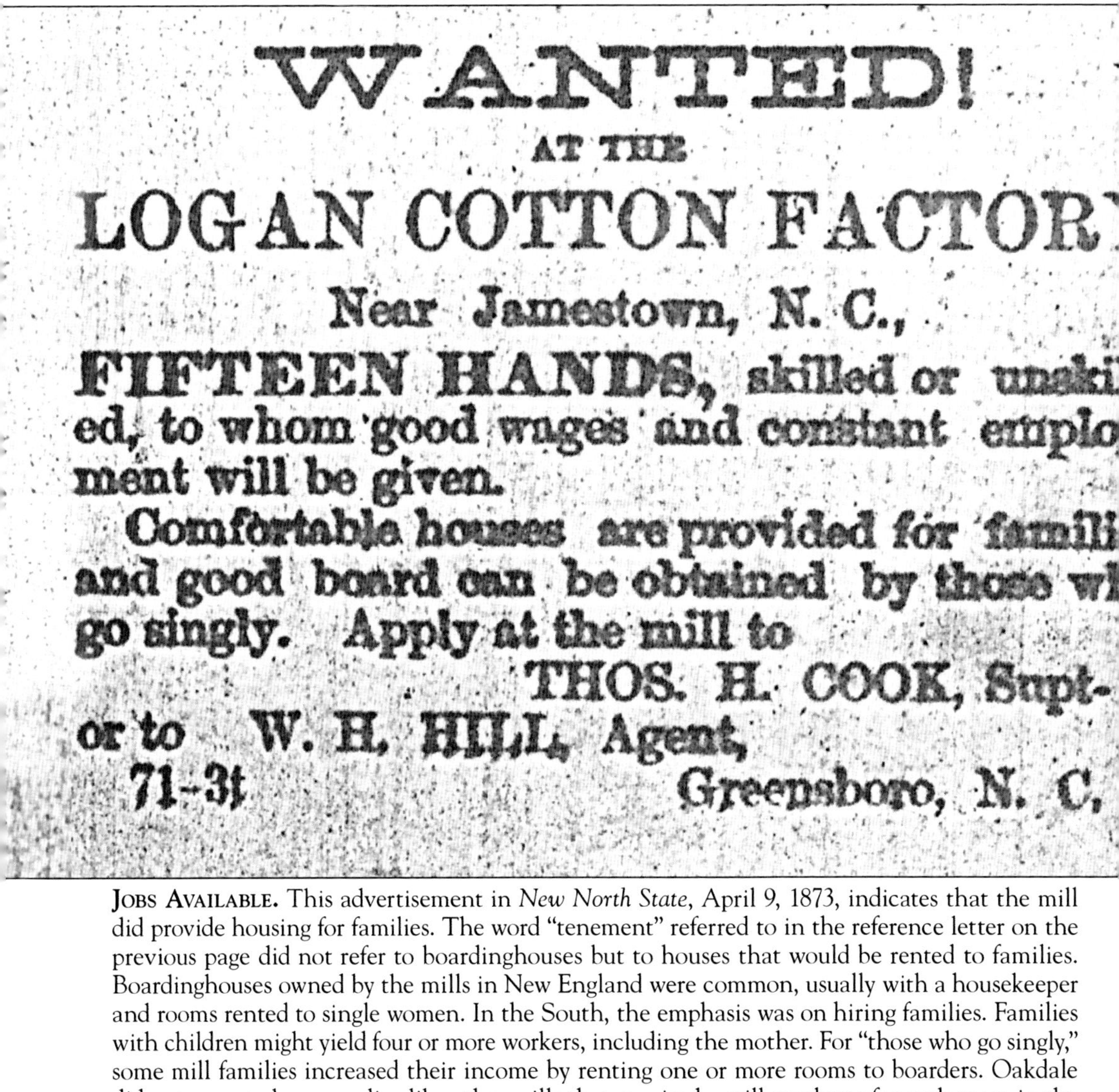

WANTED!

AT THE

LOGAN COTTON FACTOR

Near Jamestown, N. C.,

FIFTEEN HANDS, skilled or unski
ed, to whom good wages and constant emplo
ment will be given.

Comfortable houses are provided for famili
and good board can be obtained by those wh
go singly. Apply at the mill to

THOS. H. COOK, Supt.

or to W. H. HILL, Agent,

71-3t Greensboro, N. C.

Jobs Available. This advertisement in *New North State*, April 9, 1873, indicates that the mill did provide housing for families. The word "tenement" referred to in the reference letter on the previous page did not refer to boardinghouses but to houses that would be rented to families. Boardinghouses owned by the mills in New England were common, usually with a housekeeper and rooms rented to single women. In the South, the emphasis was on hiring families. Families with children might yield four or more workers, including the mother. For "those who go singly," some mill families increased their income by renting one or more rooms to boarders. Oakdale did not seem to have a policy like other mills that required a mill employee for each room in the house. The advertisement for 15 hands, skilled or unskilled, gives some indication of the size of the operation at this time. Logan Cotton Factory changed the name on its product tags to Oakdale Mills in 1871, prior to changing the name of the business to Oakdale Cotton Mills in 1894.

EARLY MILL AND VILLAGE. The rural setting of the mill and village is apparent in this April 1886 photograph. A few mill houses can be seen at left, above a single-story mill building. The early group of houses were two stories and larger than many typical mill houses. At least one house or barn is at the top of the ridge, close to the road to Jamestown. Some hands may have lived in the gold mining camp nearby, while others, especially daughters of area farmers, lived at home or boarded with local families. By 1885, the workforce had grown to 80—60 of which were women. The rhythm of the planting and harvesting seasons kept some workers away from the mill for a time, and that seemed acceptable to management that needed experienced workers. Highs and lows of the river caused the mill to shut down periodically, providing workers an unpaid respite from the 12-hour weekdays and 10-hour Saturdays.

Early Residents. Quakers Henry "Hooter" Hodgin and his wife, Rachel Irwin, first lived along Deep River below the mill. Rachel is said to have washed clothes in the river and dried them on the rocks on the bank. Furniture and other household items were homemade. Henry worked at the mill as a maintenance man, but he also had a farm in Sumner Township where he and his children worked during planting and harvesting seasons. Henry and most of his 12 children worked at the mill at some time, and grandchildren and their spouses followed. The family lived in this house on the hill facing the side of the mill after Henry died in 1889. Pictured above from left to right are Charlie Hodgin, nephew Herbert Hodgin (the child at his feet), housekeeper Mag Archie (in the doorway), seated matriarch Rachel Hodgin, Nan Hodgin, Annie Hodgin, and John Henry Hodgin, Charlie's twin. John Henry and Charlie started careers at the mill helping their father when they were about 12 years old, a year before their father died in 1889. (Mary Ann Hodgin.)

Dressed for the Camera. Pictured are, from left to right, (first row) Alice Wood (Washam), Charlie Young, May Young, and Floyd Young, who became major league baseball player "Pepper" Young; (second row) Julia Stevenson Wood, James Wood, Bertie Phillips Young, John Young, Venney Miller, and Mary Stevenson. John Young worked in the mill for 60 years and was the village barber. The Youngs had 11 children. This building continues to be referred to as the boardinghouse, but there were no boardinghouses as such in the village. However, Oakdale families did take in boarders. It is not clear if either the Wood or Young family lived in this building or if it was a convenient place to pose for a photograph. The stairs at the right have been removed, and what had been a door at the head of the stairs has been partially boarded up and is now a window. (Allison Wood.)

Out for a Ride. Ima Young and her brother, Ivan "Shorty" Young, two of the 11 children of John and Bertie Young, are ready for a rough ride in 1912. Mill records show that Ima Young (Burns), her sisters Lola (Burns) and Lucy (Loflin), brother Floyd, and their father were all employed by Oakdale in 1955. Families often stayed in the village for generations and married within the village community. (Norma Cruthis.)

Not Ready to Smile. Van Farrington, son of Albert and Luvenia Farrington, and Ima Young, daughter of John and Bertie Young, were among the many children in the village in the early 1900s. Since many mothers worked at the mill, children were often cared for by women and girls who worked a different shift. An alternative was for parents to work different shifts. (Norma Cruthis.)

SINGING FOR THE LORD. From left to right, Adela Reeves Laster; her mother, Rebecca Reeves; and Adela's mother-in-law, Molly Laster practice a song for a tent meeting near the mill in the early 1900s. Thomas Cook's diary entry for August 2, 1874, comments on an earlier meeting: "There has been quite a revival going on amongst the factory people for the past week or ten days." (Helen Laster Chambers.)

HE CAME COURTING. William Henry Reeves, a 45-year-old Civil War veteran, married 18-year-old Oakdale spooler Rebecca Loyal around 1886, despite her conclusion that he was an old man. They worked at Oakdale until at least 1910. Henry and Becky left Oakdale and moved to nearby Greensboro to work at Pomona Cotton Mill. Henry is buried in abandoned Old Pomona Cotton Mill cemetery. (Helen Laster Chambers.)

By the Old Mill Stream. From left to right are Julia Stevenson, Mary Stevenson, unidentified, Walter Stevenson, Cordelia Stevenson, Alvah Stevenson, Alice Phillips Stevenson, and Henry Stevenson. The house still stands below the mill on the bank of the mill pond, perhaps the largest of the original houses. What appears to be an addition to the house, seen at the right rear, may have been a kitchen. The mill history lists a number of floods over the years, and this house, so close to the river, probably did not escape the water's reach. Henry was a farmer, and descendants tell that he did work at the mill, but he may have continued to farm as well. Partially transcribed monthly time books list Alvah and Mary Stevenson employed in the mill in 1906 and beyond. A Cora Stevenson is listed in 1912, possibly Cordelia. Julia married James Wood, and she and Mary appear on a previous page with the Young and Wood families. (Allison Wood.)

The Way It Was. Esther Leonard Proctor, son Clayton, and Curtis "Curt" Proctor pose for the photographer. Curtis Proctor is listed in the 1906 employee time book when he was 10. Esther began spinning at 16. Curt worked in the carding room, and he and Esther married at the carding room window while Curt worked his shift. Esther and the preacher stood outside. Shifts were 12 hours long, 10 on Saturdays, leaving little time for a wedding. Another son, Coy, reported that their first house contained three rooms, but they moved several times to larger quarters. Kerosene lamps provided light, clothes were washed by hand with water "toted" from the well, and a flat iron was heated on the wood stove. Broom straw was fashioned into a broom to sweep the yard to keep grass from growing. Shoes were repaired with worn leather belts from mill machinery. Curt made home brew, put the jars in a sack, and stashed it in the river to keep it cold. Other workers did the same. (Coy Proctor.)

Wake-Up Call. The bell that wakened workers at 5:00 a.m. and rang again at 5:30 a.m. hung in the monitor at the top of the tower. It would ring for the third time at 6:00 a.m., when workers were to be at their stations. A steam whistle was eventually installed on the roof to waken workers and to announce shift changes. When World War II ended, the whistle rope was tied down so the whistle would blow until the steam ran out.

Marking the End. The bell was removed from the tower recently in preparation for the mill closing. It dates to at least 1889 when the tower was completed; there is no marker's mark to verify an earlier date. When Franklin D. Roosevelt died in 1945, the bell was rung; it may also have been rung when William G. Ragsdale died in 1929.

The Well. Initially, the well near the mill property entrance was the single source of water for drinking, cooking, and bathing for village families. The mule teams were watered there as well. Other wells were dug or drilled as the size of the village grew. Men gathered at the well in the evenings to talk until it was time to call it a day, often by 9:00 or earlier.

Water Problems. In August 1915, William G. Ragsdale's son Willie was diagnosed with typhoid fever. Water from Ragsdale's dug well proved to be contaminated, and other family members were vaccinated. The report from the health department stated that many dug wells in the area had similar problems. Another sample was to be tested in three days after treating the well with chemicals. (RC.)

Water Problems Continue. Sam Ham worked in the mill for 50¢ a day in 1912. Sam contracted typhoid fever and died at 23 in August 1919. He had a small savings account and apparently had paid into a burial association. His savings covered his board and a bill at the local store. William Ragsdale instructed the funeral home to bill the balance of the burial expenses to him. (RC.)

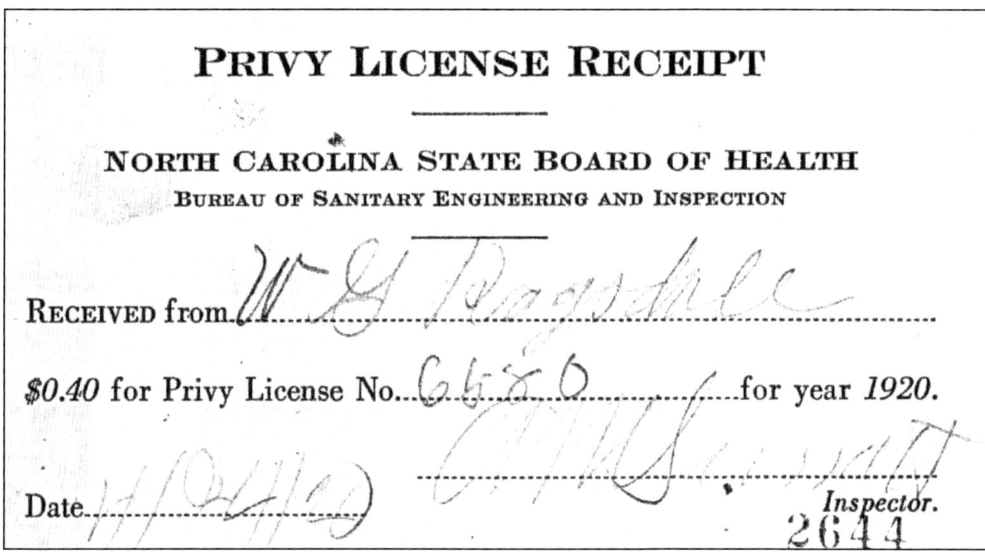

PRIVY LICENSE RECEIPT

NORTH CAROLINA STATE BOARD OF HEALTH

BUREAU OF SANITARY ENGINEERING AND INSPECTION

RECEIVED from W G Ragsdale

$0.40 for Privy License No. 6580 for year *1920.*

Date 11/24/20

Inspector.

2644

Attacking the Problem. In July 1919, North Carolina passed a law requiring every residence located within 300 yards of another residence to have an improved privy of the type approved by the State Board of Health. Typhoid, dysentery, and diarrheal diseases of infants were often caused by seepage into wells from outhouses. This privy may have been in the village, perhaps near the well. (RC.)

Other Times, Other Uses. The small white building was once the village barbershop. Windows on each side provided light; a woodstove provided warmth. Men gathered there to talk and play music. John "Babe" Young was the barber. When the building was no longer used for a barbershop, George Hodgin moved it to the back of his village home, where it was used for a wash house. (Barbara Morgan.)

The Cruthis Family. From left to right are James William "Will" Cruthis, son Hillery Cruthis holding Mary Ann Crews, and Will's wife, Bettie Cox Modlin Cruthis. Based on available company records, Will and children Callie, Robert, Hillery, and Raymond worked in the mill. Hillery was well known for cutting hair on Saturday nights in a room off his front porch. Whole families came to visit and play with Hillery's seven children while the men got their hair cut. Hillery had a green thumb and planted vegetable gardens in backyards where the resident did not intend to garden. The resident could take fresh vegetables from the garden, but the bulk of the crop was canned by Hillery's wife, Emily Edwards Cruthis, about 500 jars of vegetables, jellies, and fruits every summer. Many of the villagers raised hogs, including Hillery, and he killed hogs and cleaned them for $2 each. He was an enterprising fellow who worked hard in the mill and out. (Patricia Hatfield.)

At the Wood Pile. From left to right are (first row) Peggy Crews and Ray and Dallas Hutchinson; (second row) Shirley Cruthis, Cecil Jones, and Betty Jones. The mill operated a wood and coal yard, and employees could buy fuel at cost for fireplaces and wood stoves. The mill delivered wood near the buyer's home, and he cut the wood to size. The three boys in the photograph worked in the mill when they were older. Cecil Jones played on the mill baseball team and was a member of the winning team that participated in a fishing tournament sponsored by a textile industry organization in 1993. At that time, he had worked at the mill for 37 years. Two of the little girls in the photograph are wearing shoes, while the other children are bare-footed, probably as usual. There is no date for this photograph, but note the vintage automobile in the left rear. (Patricia Hatfield.)

Early to Work. Janie Sullivan Davis, born in 1881, began working as a spinner at Oakdale at age 12. She married Charles Davis, a farmer, and continued at the mill. When their daughter, Addline, was a youngster, her father drove her to the mill in the summer. She climbed in a window there and helped her mother in the spinning room. Janie was the only mill worker in her family. (Addline Davis Hill.)

Family Photograph. Pictured here in the village, Lula Modlin Hutchinson; her husband, Oscar; and sons Ray (left) and Dallas Hutchinson lived in the house next to the mill. Lula and Oscar both worked in the mill, Lula as a spinner and Oscar as a doffer. Both boys worked in the mill when they were older. Only employees were eligible to live in the village until a few years ago. (Patricia Hatfield.)

FARM LIFE AT THE MILL. Harlan Young introduced son Jimmy to another side of village life at an early age. Many families kept chickens, hogs, and a cow. When Jimmy got older, he started to work at the mill part-time in 1956, then full-time from 1959 to 1969, following in the footsteps of his father; his mother, Esther Breedlove; two grandmothers; and a grandfather. (Jimmy Young.)

AT HOME IN THE VILLAGE. Three-room houses were added to the village, a contrast to the roomier early housing. Jimmy Young and cousin Runell Harville stand in front of the Young home. When electricity became available, it was limited to a single lightbulb hanging from the ceiling in each room. Initially, there were no screens or screen doors, and flypaper and fly spray were popular.

Wash Day in the Village. Water for washing clothes had to be brought from the well and heated, either on the woodstove or outside in a black iron kettle over an open fire. Clothes were wrung out by hand and hung in the yard to dry. Many women made lye soap, which was hard on clothes and skin alike.

The Good Earth. From early days in the village, almost everyone planted a vegetable garden in the backyard and canned the harvest to get through the winter. Here family members plant potatoes in Farris "Sonny" and Barbara Morgan's garden. At one time, villagers would sell fresh produce from their abundance to the village store or to neighbors. Sometimes, the surplus was simply given to neighbors. (Barbara Morgan.)

WELL-DESERVED REST. Twins John Henry Hodgin (forefront) and Charlie Hodgin relax after long careers at the mill. As boys, they each had mill responsibilities. John Henry carried water for brick masons rebuilding the main structure. He also lighted and tended kerosene lamps on the night shift and oiled spinning room machines. Charlie carried wood from the basement for the woodstoves that heated the mill and tended the stoves. Their parents were Quakers and attended meeting regularly. Singing was part of their family entertainment, but playing cards and dancing were forbidden. The twins went off to barn dances anyway, young men testing their independence. John Henry said that Charlie liked to dance, but he just liked looking around. He met his wife at a barn dance. Before they each married, John Henry told that Charlie liked to flirt in the mill, but John Henry just kept doing his job. (Mary Ann Hodgin.)

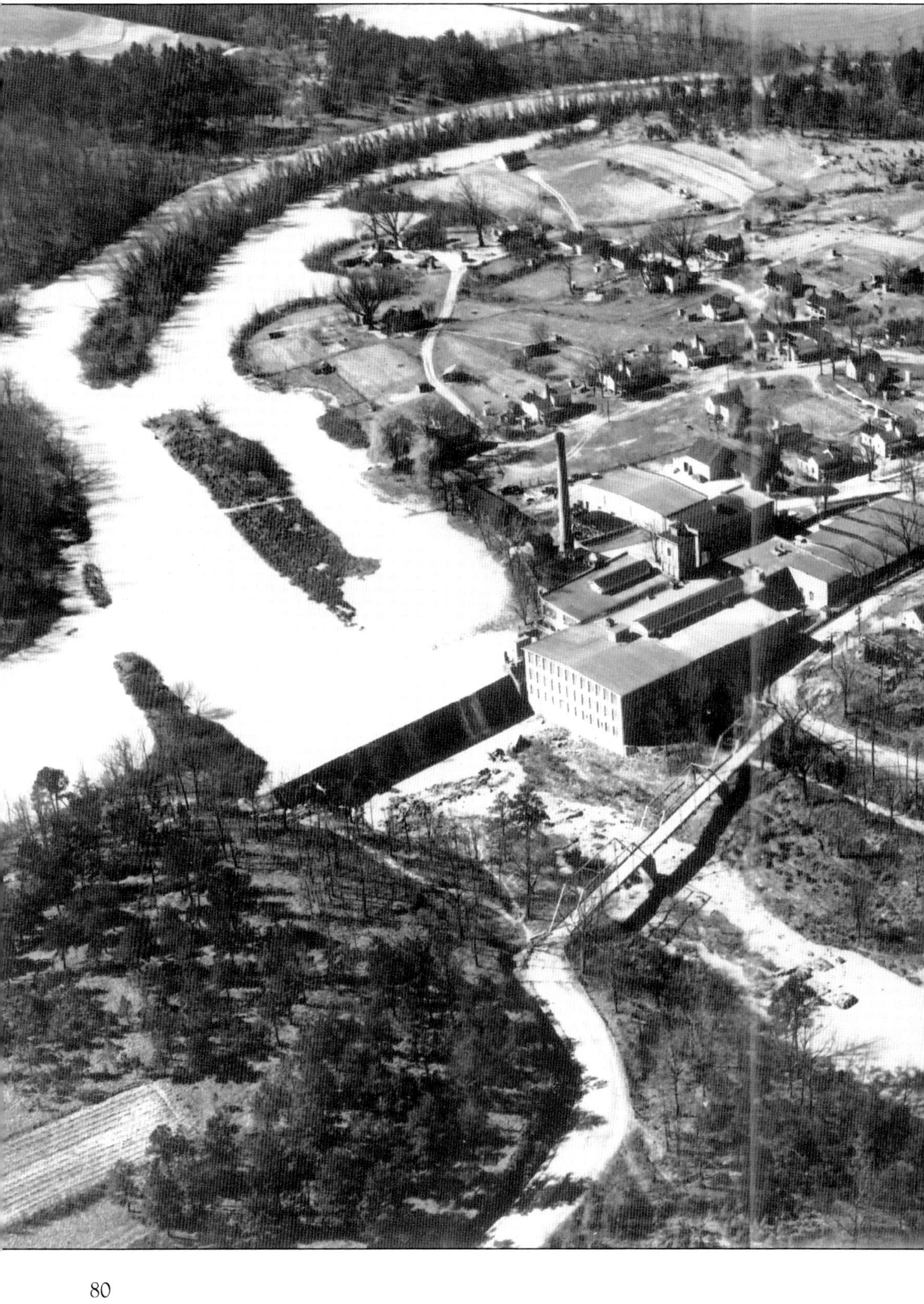

Mill Homes. The National Register of Historic Places Inventory-Nomination Form for Oakdale Cotton Mills Village reported in 1975 that there were 36 frame houses and a one-story brick store in the village. Many houses are two-story with a one-story kitchen wing. Some three-room, single-story houses have had one or more additions. Over the years, houses have burned down and lots remained vacant. There were six mill-owned houses on the far side of the bridge that were occupied by employees, set apart from the village proper. Outbuildings included chicken coops, hog pens, privies, and smokehouses. The tail race can be seen emerging from the back of the mill and joining Bull Run Creek as it flows toward Deep River. This photograph dates from around 1945. (Photograph by Fairchild Aerial Surveys, Inc.)

Should I Play with Him? Teresa Proctor stands at the side of a mill house whose underpinnings look precariously stacked. Some houses stood above ground at the front or back, so much so in some cases that a person could stand upright beneath the house. Children played there, and the space was used for storage for tools and potatoes limed to hold over the winter. (Coy Proctor.)

A Very Handy Man. Glenn Vick, the mill carpenter, did repair work in the mill, on the village houses, and on the superintendent's house. During the 1950s, he underpinned all of the village houses, closing off access to space underneath. For the children that meant the loss of favorite play spaces. Vick also paneled rooms inside many of the houses. (Patricia Vick Cruthis.)

More Things to Buy. At the dawn of the 20th century, this site in the village was being prepared for Oakdale Store. Construction began in June 1901, and the store still stands at the corner of Oakdale Road and Oak Street, a stone's throw from the mill. A company store existed somewhere in the village prior to this, the earliest record appearing in an 1868–1894 ledger that reports the inventory. It depicts a general merchandise store for a rural area where the customers' needs included a wide variety of items such as hardware, house wares, dry goods, notions, packaged and dry food, and many other items needed in the course of daily living. It was common for mill owners to provide a store for their employees, and purchases were charged against earnings, so the pay envelope on payday may have been very slight, depending on the needs of the employee and his or her family. Families worked hard planting and raising chickens and hogs so they would need to buy only staples like flour, sugar, and coffee.

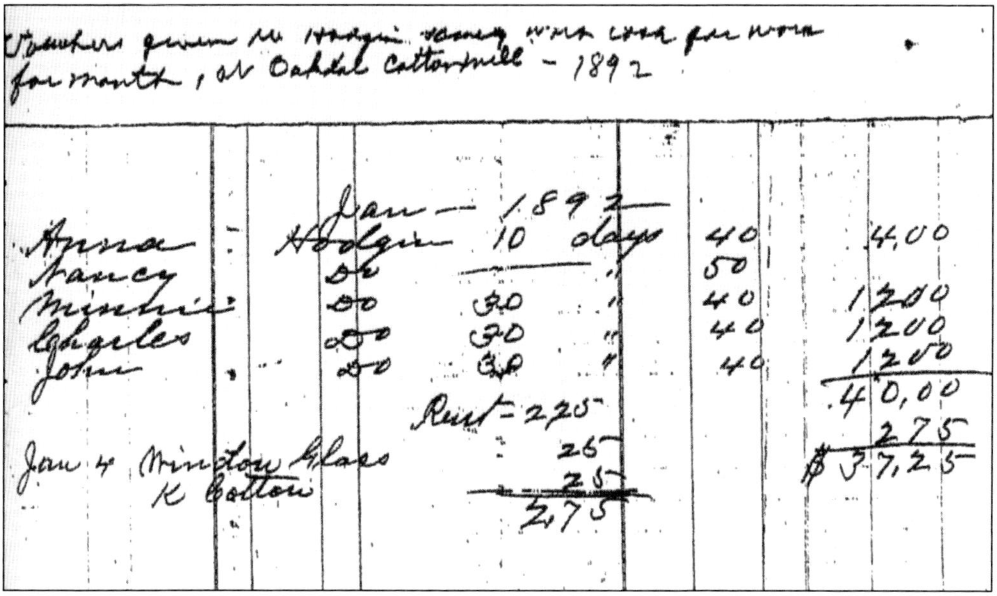

Vouchers given to Hodgin family with cash for work for month, at Oakdale Cotton Mill – 1892

		Jan – 1892		
Anna	Hodgin	10 days	40	4.00
Nancy	Do	"	50	
Minnie	Do	30 "	40	12.00
Charles	Do	30 "	40	12.00
John	Do	30 "	40	12.00
				40.00
		Rent – 225		275
Jan 4	Window Glass	25		$37.25
	K Cotton	25		
		275		

Rent Deductions. The monthly account above reads, "Vouchers given to Hodgin Family with cash for work for month at Oakdale Cotton Mill—1892," reads the ledger above. Deductions included January rent—$2.25 for the mill-owned house they rented—and 50¢ for window glass and cotton bought at the store. If the three youngest children, Charles, John, and Minnie, actually worked 30 days in January, they would have had only one day off in a month.

Early Image of Store Entrance. Oscar Patterson and Everett LaMar ran Oakdale Store at one time. The store's ledger illustrates the range of items available—drugs, groceries, notions, yard goods, clothing, furniture, hardware, and feed for chickens, hogs, and cows. The store also functioned as a bank of sorts, giving small amounts of cash to individuals who were owed money and charging it to the debtor's account. The owners never charged interest.

A Friendly Place. Although not clearly visible in this photograph, when white paint with gray trim was added to the store years before, only the front of the store was painted. The store was a gathering place for men of the village, who sat around the potbelly stove discussing problems of the day and playing a bit of music. Vending machines attest to the currency of this photograph.

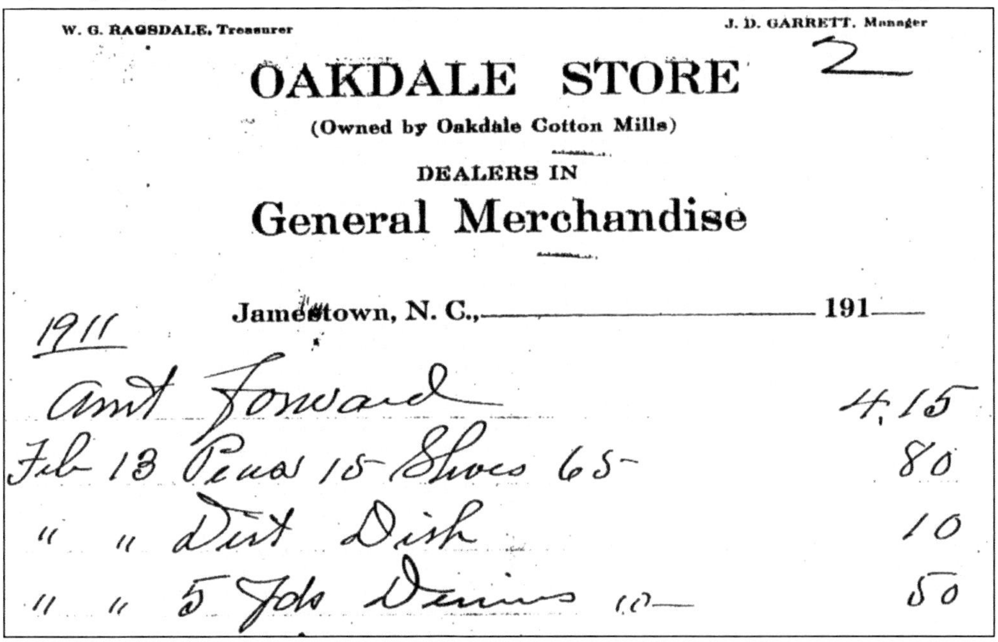

W. G. RAGSDALE, Treasurer — J. D. GARRETT, Manager

2

OAKDALE STORE

(Owned by Oakdale Cotton Mills)

DEALERS IN

General Merchandise

Jamestown, N. C., 191

1911

Amt Forward	4.15
Feb 13 Pecans 15 Shoes 65	80
" " Dirt Dish	10
" " 5 Yds Denim 10	50

Problems at the Store. In November 1911, J. D. Garrett, store manager, wrote to William G. Ragsdale asking for a raise to $65 per month, noting that "everything has advanced from 1/4 to 1/3 in the past 2 or 3 years." He had been promised that his wages would be increased from time to time. Ragsdale considered selling the store but decided to rent it. (RC.)

THIS IS TO CERTIFY, *That I,*..

desire............................*pounds of sugar for use in canning, preserving, or pickling fruits, and that I hereby pledge that none of the sugar purchased under this certificate will be used for any other purpose. I further agree that none of this sugar shall be sold, given, or loaned to any other individual. I declare further that the amount of sugar above stated, together with what I have on hand at present for such purposes, is not in excess of my requirements for canning, preserving, or pickling during the next 30 days.*

(Signed)..

OTHER KINDS OF PROBLEMS. During World War I, shortages of commodities led to rationing. The government recognized the importance of preserving food and provided sugar certificates for home canning. Stores may have been limited in the amount of sugar they could keep on hand. On June 29, 1918, William G. Ragsdale notified the County Food Administrator that he had on hand 25 pounds more than he was entitled to. (RC.)

FRIENDLY NEIGHBORHOOD STORE. When Jack Armstrong (left) and Truman Kiger ran the store, Armstrong's reputation for quality meats brought customers from village and town. Frank Merritt managed the store during the Depression, and Carl Bundy ran it. Bundy let mill employees have food when they could not pay for it. When Ernest Swanson operated the store in 1943, two young men attempted to rob the store, killing Swanson. Later George Dixon operated the store.

Doing Double Duty. The store had been vacant for a time when Lucy Ragsdale asked Doris and Earl Hodgin to consider renting and stocking the store. The Hodgins agreed, bought basic staples, and alternated shifts in the mill and at the store. Store hours were 8:30 a.m. to 7:00 p.m. The store was cash and carry, but Earl was known to help those in need. (Doris Hodgin.)

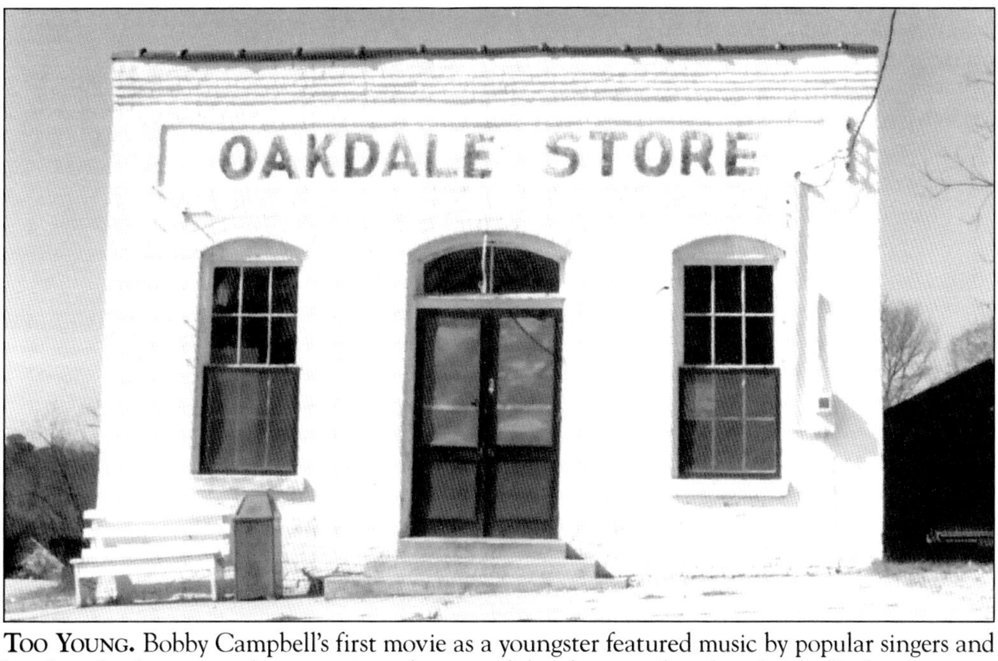

Too Young. Bobby Campbell's first movie as a youngster featured music by popular singers and bands and a short story about growing tobacco and the pleasure of smoking Lucky Strike cigarettes. It was shown on a screen mounted on the outside of the store door. Neighborhood boys and their fathers stood outside to watch. Young boys could gather discarded butts at the mill gate, so the habit developed early.

Recapturing Memories. When the store had been closed several years, Barbara Morgan proposed reopening it as a grocery store, offering staples and a gathering place for the community. Owners agreed; the mill carpenter refurbished the inside, replacing the floor and windows, and gave everything a fresh coat of pain. Barbara's husband, Farris "Sonny" Morgan, worked at the mill for 45 years. The store is part of their family history. (Barbara Morgan.)

Off to a Good Start. Barbara Morgan's motivation to reopen the store was twofold: get the community together and establish a profitable business. The decor created a country atmosphere, and the grand opening on November 15, 1986, featured square dancing to bluegrass music. A pool table, a pinball machine, and a checkerboard invited friendly competition, and video games added a modern touch. (Barbara Morgan.)

DASHED HOPES. The Recessions, with Andy Morgan (left) and Calvin Anderson, played for the grand opening. Summer 1987 was unbearable without air-conditioning. Refrigeration units ran hard to keep perishables cold. Candy melted on the shelves. Electric bills skyrocketed, and the store was forced to close. The darkened store holds years of memories—friendly conversation, impromptu fiddle or banjo music, and a sense of togetherness that permeated the village. (Barbara Morgan.)

ONLY A PLAYGROUND NOW. From left to right, Noah Morgan and C. J. Morgan, Barbara Morgan's grandsons, play in front of the padlocked store. They were too young to experience the reopening of the store. Their only knowledge of this building's past will be from stories passed down from elders who relive those days with a smile, a laugh, and a shake of the head in amusement or disbelief. (Barbara Morgan.)

OAKDALE SCHOOL, JANUARY 22, 1913. Built about 1912 or 1913 by the mill, it was considered a public school, though the mill always owned it. It was attended by children who lived in the mill village and along Harvey Road. An earlier school nearby, standing in the 1870s, was sometimes used for religious services, according to Thomas Cook, who saw to it that palings were set up around it.

OAKDALE KIDS. Oakdale School students pose in front of the schoolhouse. The only identification available is of Howard Wood on the left end of the first row. He was born in 1924 and appears to be about six years old here. Some of the teachers at Oakdale were Estelle Jones, May Jones, Fannie Ozment Reynolds, Annie Wiley, John Lindley, Amanda Leonard, Addie Boone, and Ethel Daniels. (Allison Wood.)

THE 1941 CLASS AT OAKDALE SCHOOL. For many children, this primary education was the only schooling they had. Those who continued had a long walk to the elementary school in Jamestown and were sometimes subjected to name-calling and rude behavior. The mill and village were considered the other side of the tracks, which they actually were. Some children wanted to drop out because of the atmosphere. In 1943, the school merged with Jamestown School. Although some names are missing, the students above include, from left to right, (first row) Donald Stack, Nancy Varner, Delbert Jones, Mary Lynn Hodgin, Gordon Washam, and unidentified; (second row) Mackay McClure, Joann Dunn, Delmar Brown, Tiny Breedlove, Billy Campbell, Norma Burns, and Bobby Campbell. A number of these children's names appear on mill employment records. (Jamestown Alumni Association.)

MANY MEMORIES. Howard Wood lived next to the school and remembered that his parents' home (Jim and Julia Wood) was the school's first aid station when some child was hurt. When Howard was eight or nine years old, he was hired by the county to build a fire each morning in the stove and sweep out the building. He received $5 a month for his services. (Allison Wood.)

OAKDALE SCHOOL UNDERGOING REPAIRS. Cloakrooms on either side of the door held coats, lunches, coal or wood, and a water pail, carried by two people who slipped a broomstick under the handle. A bell in the cupola rang to start school. Paper came already used on one side by students at Jamestown School, so Oakdale scholars turned the paper over to use the back. (Mary A. Browning.)

SUPERINTENDENT'S HOUSE, 1940S. When Samuel L. McClure first applied for a position as superintendent at Oakdale in 1911, he wrote that he hoped to have a house "off to its self," so that he could have some chickens and a garden. At first, he probably lived where previous superintendents had, in a house near the mill and the store. This house was built for him, probably by 1920. (RC.)

SUPERINTENDENT'S HOUSE, 2009. Margie Cruthis Coleman remembers delivering corn to Daisy McClure and being invited to swing on the porch swing. "Clete" Campbell was the next superintendent to occupy the house. He purchased it from Oakdale in 1972 and left it to Oakdale Methodist Church. The church sold it to Campbell's niece, Lois Hodgin, in 1975. Tony and Pat Cruthis purchased it in 1997 and have restored it. (Mary A. Browning.)

Oakdale United Methodist Church. Mill management endorsed religious services as a matter of conviction and prudence, providing meeting places. Thomas Cook attended area Methodist, Presbyterian, and Quaker services; invited ministers to speak at the factory and old schoolhouse; and often shortened a workday so employees could attend local revivals. This Methodist congregation first met about 1878 in a brush arbor they built about where the superintendent's house later stood. (Frederick P. Browning.)

Oakdale Methodist Congregation, 1947. In 1915, the mill gave land for a church building, and the first part of the current structure was constructed. Another Methodist group organized at Flint Hill School in New Jamestown and built a church on East Main Street. For many years, the same pastor served both churches, though one snobbish minister's wife is said to have refused to attend services at Oakdale.

Bales Memorial Wesleyan Church in 1944. This was not an official outgrowth of Oakdale Cotton Mills but was organized in 1911 by a group of Oakdale's employees, and its bell was rung when a mill village resident died. For more than 30 years, its pastor was Ernest M. Gardner, who was also a 50-year veteran fixer for Oakdale. (Addline Davis Hill.)

Bales Memorial Wesleyan Church. This brick sanctuary was begun in 1961 and extended a few years later. Just left of the picture area, the old bell was secured to a brick standard. It is said that Monroe Proctor rang the bell to signal a death, but as he got older, he sometimes rang the bell when no one had died. Jimmy Young now rings the bell every Sunday. (Mary A. Browning.)

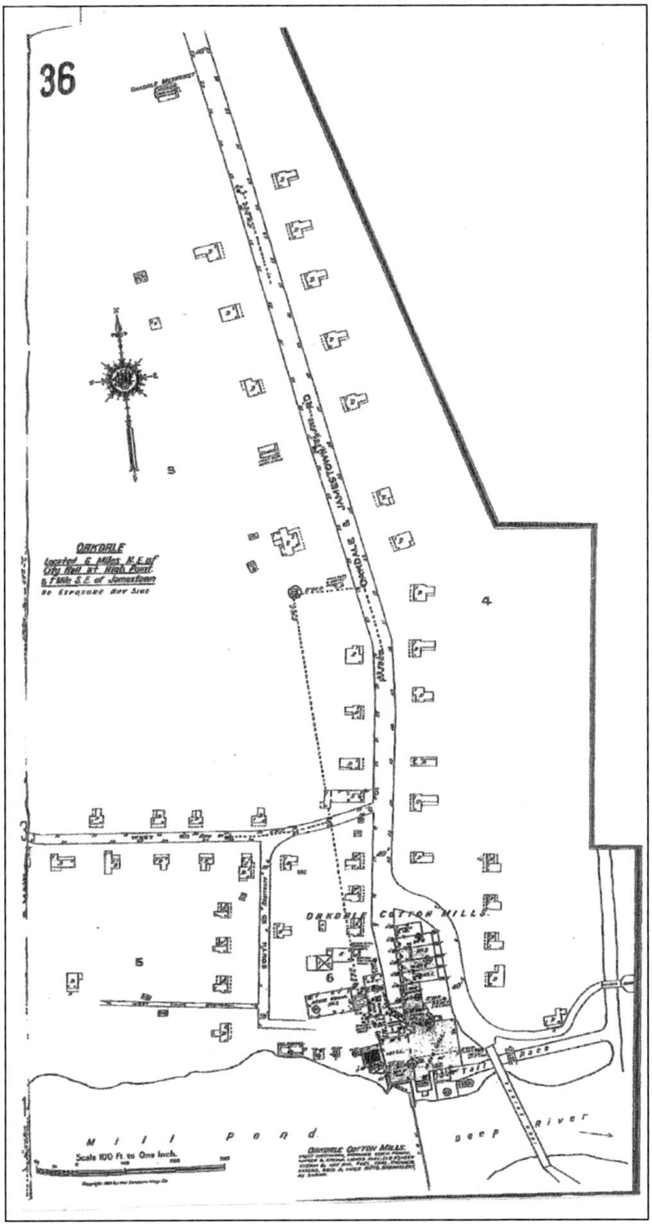

OAKDALE, 1924. The Sanborn Map Company of San Francisco made insurance maps of locations all around the country, and in 1924, their map of High Point included three locations in Jamestown: Jamestown School, Tuberculosis Sanatorium, and Oakdale Cotton Mills. At the time, Jamestown was not an incorporated municipality, but these properties were insured and needed to be mapped. This map of Oakdale is valuable for its detail, which shows all of the buildings belonging to Oakdale. It begins on the north (top) with Oakdale Methodist Church, then shows houses and a few larger outbuildings along both sides of the road, including Oakdale School and the water tower, down to the mill. The mill buildings are all shown as they were configured at that time. "Happy Holler," the old village, is shown with the existing streets. For those wanting a closer view of the map, it can be seen at the High Point Library's North Carolina Collection. (High Point Library North Carolina Collection.)

Four

Recreation, Outreach, and Celebrations

There are important matters that fall outside the workaday world of the mill. Recreation, for instance, has always been a substantial element in the lives of Oakdale people, and certain things were easily available to them that enriched their leisure time. Sports—baseball and softball especially—were passions for many. Other pastimes revolved around Deep River. The closeness of the village community meant children always had someone to play a game with. Extending beyond that world in another direction were the ways the mill and its management interacted with the larger community around it, assuming responsibilities in educational and political institutions, and in philanthropic endeavors, even taking the lead in incorporating the town of Jamestown and supplying the know-how in setting up essential public works and practical management procedures. In addition, Oakdale could nearly always be counted upon to help its own employees deal with special problems, no matter what they might be. Lastly, mill management has taken recognition of the individual worker very seriously and looked for ways to celebrate employee milestones. It is not so hard to do in a place where everybody knows everybody.

Deep River. There was endless entertainment available around the river—watching, fishing, skating, or swimming. Coy Proctor recalls one hot, sticky summer night when his dad, Curtis, suggested a cooling swim in the river. He led the kids down and into the water, but it was dark as pitch and when something unidentified made a splash nearby, the party retreated to the bank, deciding everyone was now cool enough.

Deep River Swimming Hole. Esther Young poses on the riverbank. One youngster has an inner tube, but the water does not look very deep. The more adventurous kids liked to climb high up in a tree on the bank, drop into the water, and then float downstream to the pond. Coy Proctor said there were three places to swim when he was a kid: the one for girls, the one for boys, and the one at Moore's, the mill upstream from Oakdale. (Jimmy Young.)

Going Fishing. Fishing was fun, cheap, and, with luck, provided something to add to the pinto beans and corn bread on the table. A stick, some string, and a safety pin might do the trick. Sometimes when the river was low, fish got caught behind the dam and could be grabbed right out of the water. The river could also keep corn liquor from blowing its top. Put the jar in a cloth bag and secure it in the water. That keeps it cool and out of sight.

Boat on the Mill Pond. A quiet day on the water is a great way to relax. The mill always has at least one utility work boat in place. Limon Hodgin and Hillery Cruthis had boats; others probably did as well. Margie Cruthis liked to take her father's boat down to the dam, make a U-turn, and run it back. She said she never heard of a child drowning until recent years.

DWIGHT BISHER (LEFT), JIM ROLLINS (CENTER), AND CHARLES MCDANIEL (RIGHT). Harker's Island near Beaufort was the site of this big catch. In another year, 1993, the North Carolina Textile Week Fishing Tournament was held at Carolina Beach; Oakdale's four-member team caught a fish weighing 35 pounds and 5 ounces and received a trophy that was exhibited at the mill. That team included Jeff Johnson, Cecil Jones, Charles McDaniel, and Danny McDaniel.

WILLIAM E. HODGIN FAMILY PICNIC. This image was made about 1910, possibly at a corn shucking. From left to right are Cornelia Hodgin, William "Bill" Hodgin, Martha Hodgin (later Allred), Lucy Hodgin (later Modlin), Beulah Hodgin (later Hughes), Joseph Hodgin, and Maude Hodgin Clark with a child. (Quentin Hodgin.)

GIRLS' SOFTBALL TEAM, 1946. "We were so proud of our red and white uniforms!" says Margie Cruthis Coleman, who was 14 when this team was formed. She was usually the pitcher. The girls played on a field in High Point behind the old post office. Intramural sports with school teams were also popular with mill village kids, who played all kinds of ball all the time, organized or not. (Margie Cruthis Coleman.)

OAKDALE'S GIRLS' TEAM. Shown are, from left to right, Jeanette Campbell, Lydia Hodgin, Linda Hodgin, and Shirley Wall. Other team members, not shown, were Betty Jones, Shirley Cruthis, Doris Burns, Norma Burns, Margie Cruthis, Marilyn Hodgin, Mona Leonard, and Helen Cruthis. Oakdale sponsored baseball teams for many years and helped to fuel baseball fever. Almost everyone caught it.

Floyd "Pep" or "Pepper" Young (1907–1962). Young was Jamestown's own major leaguer. He signed with the Pittsburgh Pirates as a utility infielder in 1933. In 1945, after the war, he went with the St. Louis Cardinals. His career wound down to semi-pro status as a coach and player, and in time, he returned to work at Oakdale and play in its Industrial League team. He kept in shape by running along the highway while his wife, Mable, followed in her car, says Quentin Hodgin.

Oakdale Baseball Team. The Industrial League featured teams sponsored by textile mills and furniture factories and provided warm-weather entertainment for the whole area. Team members listed on the back of this photograph were "Kennith Reaves, Orral Campbell, Richard Jones, Cecil Jones, Gerald Loflin, Joe Hodgin, Earl Hodgin, Nathan Orsborn." Bill Ragsdale had talent, too, and left a major league position when he returned to Oakdale management.

Richard Jones. One of the local stars, Jones poses at the field that Oakdale developed for its team. The field was complete with bleachers that can be seen at the left. It was behind Oakdale School, according to Bobby Campbell. Mill management would put the sides up on cotton trucks and load them with kids to take them to away games in Mooresville or Asheboro.

Just Hanging Out. Every front porch had swings, chairs, benches, and front steps occupied except during the coldest weather. Boys and girls joined in village games of kick the can, hide and seek, and dodgeball. Girls liked to play jump rope, hopscotch, and house. Boys also hunted squirrels and rabbits and skinned them with their pocketknives. The knives were used in games of "peg" or variants involving skill in throwing or flipping a pocketknife and were used to carve "pegs" for the popular game of that name. Marbles were popular with both boys and girls.

LOOKS LIKE A WINNER. A homemade vehicle gets a trial run, with the master mechanic and his assistant looking on. Mill scraps plus creativity equaled toys in the hands of parents and children. Bobbin yo-yos were a staple in the mill village. Hillery Cruthis owned a goat and made a little goat cart so his kids could ride in it. He also made a seesaw that would turn. John Henry Hodgin made tin tops and a leather ball and taught kids the game of town ball that involved kicking the ball and running the bases.

MUSIC AND DANCING ON SATURDAY NIGHTS. From left to right, Harold Hodgin, Howard Hodgin, and Hillery Cruthis pose in front of the Oakdale Store. Music used to come from the old barbershop nearby on Saturday nights, but when Hillery became the village barber, people congregated at the Cruthis home on Saturdays to get their haircuts. Spouses and children came along. When Mrs. Cruthis—Emily—sat down at the piano, the dancing started. The front yard was full of children, seven of them Cruthis's, and the house full of dancers.

MILL VILLAGE AS WINTER WONDERLAND. A laundry basket makes a fine sled with someone to pull it. Jimmy Young recalls nailing old shoes to barrel staves to make skis when he was a kid. A popular treat, snow cream, was made with the second snow of the season (never the first) in the Hillery Cruthis household. Canned milk, eggs, sugar, and vanilla were mixed in a dishpan, and a dishpan of snow was mixed in with it and served in small bowls. (Barbara Morgan.)

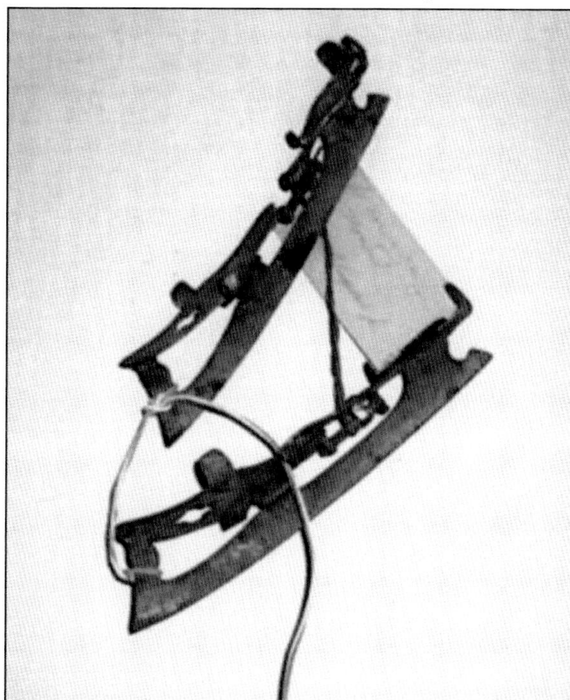

WILL'S ICE SKATES. During the time William G. Ragsdale Sr. was at Oakdale, the mill pond often froze, and blocks of ice were cut out of the frozen pond and stored in a shed near the mill. Straw was packed around the ice blocks for insulation. These skates that belonged to Will hold a place of honor in Billy Ragsdale's office in a custom-built shadowbox. (Patricia M. Koehler.)

Skating on the Oakdale Mill Pond. This beautiful old image of Robert L. Garrett skating on Oakdale's mill pond evokes another time at a familiar place. The 1920 census shows that Garrett was an engineer at the mill. (Audrey Dowdy.)

Taking a Buggy Ride. Yesterday's automobile was a fine way to get around on a warm and sunny day but not too much fun in cold weather. Buggies were made in Jamestown by brothers Benjamin F. and Henry M. Briggs in the 1860s. The family business later moved to the Florence community and then to High Point.

Going to Town. Richard Jones, Charles Jones, and Earl Hodgin walk along a busy street. There were plenty of weekend attractions in the larger towns nearby. When the fair was on in Greensboro, Sunday was the best day to go because admission was free. The cotton candy and Ferris wheel were big attractions, says Margie Cruthis Coleman. (Barbara Morgan.)

Taking a Walk. Howard and Lillian Cox Wood stroll over the bridge. This triple-span, metal Pratt truss bridge, the largest and finest in Guilford County, was built in 1922. It used to be on Oakdale Road but is now pretty well hidden by kudzu. Before the road was changed, Oakdale Road ran all the way south to Kivett Drive. Howard worked in twisting and packing and later as a carpenter. He served in the army in World War II. Lillian worked in the winding room. (Allison Wood.)

EXPLORING MCCULLOCH GOLD MILL. The neighborhood south of Oakdale once was the gold and copper mining district. The most imposing relic of that time is this building that dates from 1832, when Charles McCulloch built it to house his stationary steam engine used to crush and extract gold or copper from local ore. Little evidence of the old mines remains today. One, Deep River Mine, is under a High Point landfill.

GOLD AND COPPER. Though never extremely profitable, small mines were developed along Copper Creek by 1820 and attracted investors, prospectors, and immigrants. Even now, one might see someone panning for gold somewhere along the creek. When Oakdale Store was inventoried in 1895, something over $14 in gold bullion was listed as an asset. This building was one of several bought by Bill Ragsdale to preserve them. It has now been restored as an entertainment venue called Castle McCulloch.

Women Leaving Oakdale's Front Gate. Life does not end at the end of the work day. Nearly everyone who has worked at Oakdale can tell a story of how the mill helped out in a time of trouble. Many of these stories are about money loaned for emergencies. Some are about summer jobs for students to help pay for college. In 1995, Oakdale was certified by the Department of Labor as a provider, with Ragsdale High School, of industrial engineering apprenticeships.

First Water Tower. The tower symbolizes the many ways Oakdale has shared its experience and assets with Jamestown. The old tower, built on the highest point of mill land, dates from the 1880s. A small shed near its base stores an old pumper wagon and canvas hose. When Jamestown incorporated in 1947, the mill's experience with such matters gave the town a big advantage in organizing public works projects.

Water Filtering Plant. In September 1947, Oakdale began operating this water filtering plant. It could filter 150,000 gallons of water per day from Deep River, but the mill needed only about 30,000 gallons. Jamestown—newly incorporated—accepted the mill's offer to provide the town's water needs. The filtration plant is still used to remove mud from river water used in the dyeing process, but drinking water now comes from Jamestown, which gets it from High Point.

Coy Proctor. Shown here with his daughter Teresa, Coy specialized in keeping the mill machinery functioning. However, when Tom Ragsdale called him in and told him he was now going to work for Jamestown, Coy went to work in town instead, becoming, in effect, the original public works department. Mayor Ragsdale wore two hats, and so did many others. (Coy Proctor.)

The Community House, 1948. This popular and fondly remembered part of the larger community was officially opened on December 23, 1948, in the expansive postwar era. The structure was dedicated as a memorial to the women who had "kept the home fires burning," according to the official program. The women had also helped to keep the factory humming. The building was constructed by R. K. Stewart, using vertical oak logs cut on mill property. (Emily Ragsdale; photograph by Snow Studio.)

Grand Opening. The Community House was intended for use by everyone in the community, townsfolk as well as mill villagers. Many organizations used the upstairs meeting rooms: Rotary Club, Boy Scouts, American Legion, Junior Order, garden clubs, and many others. Gordon Dillon recalled that Oakdale sponsored Boy Scout Troup 18 at one time, paying all the dues, buying all the uniforms, and sending all members to Camp Uhwarrie for a week.

The Lounge. Movies were shown at least once a week at the Community House. There were board games and magazines on hand. The building burned to the ground in 1955, apparently because of an explosion in its oil-fired furnace. The massive chimney stood to mark the location for many years but has since been demolished. The building was a real community treasure.

Harry Jeffers. He had been a maintenance man at the mill but was recruited to practice his sideline as a first-class chef at the Community House for groups that wanted meals. The first one he fixed was a sandwich supper for the Rotary Club, according to a *Jamestown News* interview. His fried chicken was famous. He used chickens from his own farm, but, like the Colonel, he kept the actual recipe a closely guarded secret.

Community House Deck. The building was on Oakdale Road, but this broad deck on the back faced the woods and Bull Run Creek. From left to right, Joe Hodgin, Monroe Campbell, Robert Jones, Howard Hodgin, and Henry Wood are shown enjoying a quiet moment.

Atha Wright. Wright was the manager of the Community House and lived in an apartment in the building with her husband, Clem. She had worked for the county extension service, so she brought her skills in what used to be called home economics—cooking, budgeting, nutrition, and menu planning—to share with women in the community through classes and related services. A literacy program was also offered.

SUPERVISORS' MEETING AT THE COMMUNITY HOUSE. From left to right are (first row) Howard Wood, Sam Strickland, Cletus Campbell, and Limon Hodgin; (second row) Earl Hodgin, Hillery Cruthis, Harold Hodgin, Robert Jones, Monroe Campbell, and Tom Ragsdale Sr.; (third row) Howard Hodgin and Joe Hodgin. Most of these men also served as members of either Jamestown's town council or volunteer fire department.

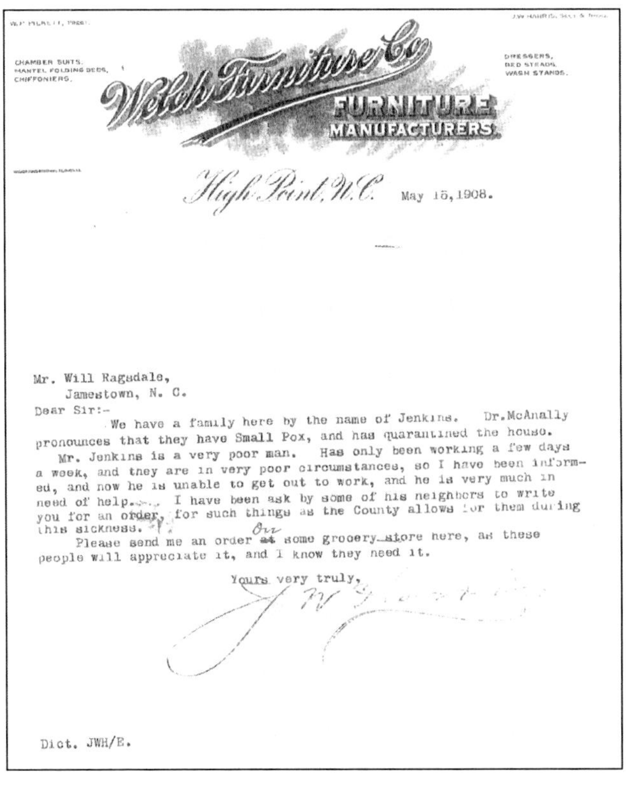

CHAMBER SUITS.
MANTEL FOLDING BEDS,
CHIFFONIERS.

Welch Furniture Co.
FURNITURE MANUFACTURERS.

DRESSERS,
BED STEADS,
WASH STANDS.

High Point, N.C. May 15, 1908.

Mr. Will Ragsdale,
Jamestown, N. C.

Dear Sir:-

We have a family here by the name of Jenkins. Dr.McAnally pronounces that they have Small Pox, and has quarantined the house.

Mr. Jenkins is a very poor man. Has only been working a few days a week, and they are in very poor circumstances, so I have been informed, and now he is unable to get out to work, and he is very much in need of help. I have been ask by some of his neighbors to write you for an order, for such things as the County allows for them during this sickness.

Please send me an order on some grocery store here, as these people will appreciate it, and I know they need it.

Yours very truly,

Dict. JWH/E.

RAGSDALE COLLECTION DOCUMENT. Will Ragsdale's many obligations are evident in this collection of business and personal records. This one, from J. W. Harris of High Point, asks for help for the Jenkins family, who had smallpox and were in very "poor circumstances." It says, "Send me an order on some grocery store here. . . . I know they need it." As head of the school committee, Ragsdale also received teachers' job applications and arranged for housing. (RC.)

County Commissioners Petition. Many of High Point's prominent citizens signed this petition urging Commissioner Ragsdale to act on their behalf in allowing Ringling Brothers Circus to exhibit in High Point in 1908. Ragsdale served in a variety of public offices, and his descendants have carried on that tradition.

TO THE HONORABLE BOARD COUNTY COMMISSIONERS
GUILFORD COUNTY, NORTH CAROLINA.

We the following citizens of High Point township respectfully petition your honorable body to recind your action in so far as High Point township is affected, in refusing permission for RINGLING BROTHERS' CIRCUS to exhibit in Guilford County during the period from Oct 1st. to 20th. 1908. We beg that the above circus be permitted to exhibit at High Point as originally planned and we further beg that prompt action in the matter be taken by your honorable body.

NAMES	NAMES
[illegible]	[illegible]
E. A. Snow	[illegible]
[illegible]	[illegible]
A. S. Parker	J. A. Marsh
W. E. Herndon	G. A. Ausband
[illegible]	[illegible]
[illegible]	W. G. Brown
W. G. Bradshaw	[illegible]
[illegible]	[illegible]
[illegible]	[illegible]
[illegible]	G. F. Duncan
[illegible]	[illegible]
[illegible]	[illegible]
[illegible]	[illegible]
[illegible]	F. Harris & Bro.

GREENSBORO, N. C., ____________191__

Mr. W. G. Ragsdale, Jamestown, N. C.

TO C. W. BANNER, M. D., DR.

PRACTICE LIMITED TO

EYE, EAR, NOSE AND THROAT

OFFICE BANNER BUILDING

Aug	2	To one new lens for Mrs. R.	1	25
Sep	7	" Ex. Eyes for Willie Sapp, col	5	00
"	"	" 1 pair gl " " "	3	75
			10	00

Received Payment
C W Banner

10-9-'16.

Glasses for Willie Sapp. This statement from Dr. C. W. Banner indicates that the doctor provided a new lens for Lucy C. Ragsdale's glasses and conducted an eye examination for "Willie Sapp, col." and made a pair of glasses for him.

Retirement Was a Long Time Coming. Esther McGee's bookkeeping career at Oakdale began by 1906 when she was 21 years old, probably about when this photograph was taken. She retired at the age of 80, wearing the same sweet smile she had in this early photograph. Retirement celebrations are special at Oakdale, each one important to the retiree and to the coworkers.

Odell Campbell. Campbell is one of those surnames that pops up often in Oakdale history. Many of the families who have worked at the mill over the years are related by marriage to many others with histories as long or longer in the mill community. A substantial spread of food went along with this gathering—another Oakdale tradition for retiring employees.

HENRY PRINCE IS HONORED. Billy Ragsdale, on the left, energizes the gathering here to recognize Henry Prince, who worked at the mill part-time during the 1970s and 1980s.

JIMMY CRUTHIS RETIRED. Jimmy also bore a name familiar to those who know the mill's history. He was the son of Raymond M. Cruthis and a nephew of Hillery Cruthis, mentioned elsewhere in this book. He began working in the mill in 1956. He is shown here with Tommy Ragsdale (left) and Billy Ragsdale (right).

Admiring the Gold Watch. Colleen Hines was presented with the traditional retirement gift of a watch. Like other retirees, she continued to receive the special Christmas treat each year, long past retirement. These small celebrations help to compensate for the repetitive nature of most mill work.

Happy Birthday Daniel Vernon. Here is an edible birthday card for Daniel and plenty of friends and coworkers around to help him eat it.

Willard Newman's Birthday. Newman went to work for Oakdale in 1964, during its most productive time. These parties helped to make going to work a little more interesting. The birthday boy seems to be enjoying it, anyway.

A Feast. The occasion is uncertain, but the place looks familiar, and the food really looks good. When foreign competition is creeping over the horizon, and the future looks uncertain, a nice spread like this can't go wrong.

Pocahontas Seeks Treats. She looks a little young to be an employee, but maybe she received a special permit to join in the fun at the mill. This celebratory innovation at Oakdale was the Halloween costume event.

Minnie Waves on Halloween. Possibly she (he?) works in one of those offices just off that hallway. She looks friendly anyway.

BOZO AT WORK ON HALLOWEEN. Who is minding the store, here, anyhow? Is this any way to run a factory? The answer, of course, is yes, this is a pretty good way to run a factory.

AN ESCAPED CONVICT. This lady—whoever she might be—is enjoying her coffee break and getting some attention, too. She does not look very dangerous.

RIDING LAWN MOWER. The special event here seems to be showing off the mill's new riding lawn mower. At the time, it was quite an innovation. The mill's photograph files also have a picture of another important innovation: a microwave oven in the break room.

ROSE ARBOR. Providing a place to stop and smell the roses, Oakdale management installed this nice rose arbor near the welding shop and oil house.

Sorting Apples for Christmas Treats. There is nothing new about this. For many years, Oakdale has given to each mill family a bag filled with fruits, candies, and peanuts at the Christmas season. These gifts were especially appreciated in the early days when fruit was scarce in winter and sweets were dear. In recent years, toys were given to the children, too. Another innovation at the mill was a Christmas club that enabled workers to put money aside for the holidays or for other special needs.

Mill Christmas Party, 1992. Oakdale went all-out at Christmastime, with two days of parties to celebrate this successful year. The Jamestown Friends Meeting catered meals for all shifts, and Santa (Larry Trent) appeared in person. As early as 1870, Oakdale gave Christmas gifts to employees. In 1909, it had a tree decorated with treats for "children of your mill operators," according to a letter from Casella Color Company of Atlanta, which contributed to the event.

Perfect Attendance Awards, 1990. Shown are, from left to right, (first row) Deloris Gardner, Harold Cruthis, and Howard Ellis; (second row) Nelda Breedlove, Shirley Parnell, Helen Hall, Wayne Greeson, Daniel Vernon, and Kevin Jones; (third row) Dewey H. Grant, Edward Twisdale, Cecil Jones, Lester Newman, and Sonny Morgan; (fourth row) Donald Carter, Thomas Gann, and Earl Hodgin. Not pictured are Sharon Hedgecock and Esther Thompson.

Potluck Supper. With spools of cotton making a suitable background in a very familiar place, Oakdale employees prepare to feast.

A Thank-You Note. Ed Allred's children thank Mr. and Mrs. William G. Ragsdale for gifts, including dolls for Nora and Bessie. The note is not dated but was filed with other papers dated from about 1914 in the Ragsdale Collection. (RC.)

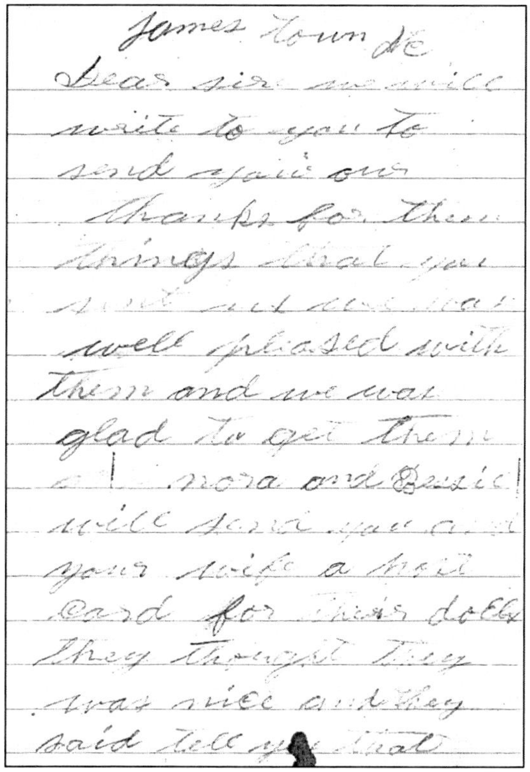

James Town NC
Dear sir we will
write to you to
send you our
thanks for them
things that you
sent us we was
well pleased with
them and we was
glad to get them
[illegible] nora and Bessie
will send you and
your wife a post
card for their dolls
They thought they
was nice and they
said tell you that

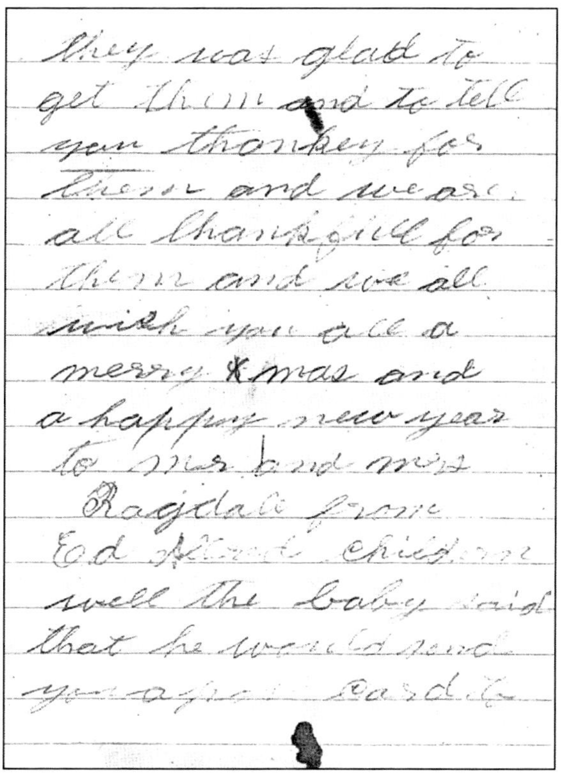

they was glad to
get them and to tell
you thankey for
them and we are
all thankfull for
them and we all
wish you all a
merry Xmas and
a happy new year
to mr and mrs
Ragsdale from
Ed Allred children
well the baby said
that he would send
you a post card [illegible]

The Allreds. The first members of the Allred family emigrated from England to Jamestown to work in the mines in the 19th century. Ed Allred was working at Oakdale by 1908. The Ragsdales may not have received many written thank-yous, but they surely got lots of verbal ones, since, from all accounts, the mill workers felt genuine affection as well as respect for them and for their successors. (RC.)

SELECT BIBLIOGRAPHY

Browning, Mary A. *Historical Places In and Around Jamestown, N.C.* Jamestown, NC: self-published, 2008.

———. *Remembering Old Jamestown: A Look Back at the Other South.* Charleston, SC: History Press, 2008.

Crouch, Esther Kersey. *A Short History of Jamestown, North Carolina.* Jamestown, NC: self-published, 1965.

Dalton, Mary. *Oakdale Cotton Mills: Close-Knit Neighbors.* (DVD) Jamestown, NC: Historic Jamestown Society, 2009.

Hall, Jacquelyn Dowd, et al. *Like A Family: The Making of a Southern Cotton Mill World.* New York: W. W. Norton, 1987.

Haney, Mary Jane. *Oakdale United Methodist Church.* Jamestown, NC: self-published, 1978.

Historic Architecture Inventory: Guilford County, North Carolina 1996. Greensboro, NC: Guilford County Historic Preservation Commission, 1996.

Hughes, Fred. *Guilford County, N.C.: A Map Supplement.* Jamestown, NC: self-published, 1988.

Jenkins, Bradford L. "Oakdale: A Southern Cotton Mill and its People, 1865–1982, a study done for NEH Summer Seminar under Prof. John Shelton Reid, UNC."

Koehler, Patricia M. "Amid Ruins, family stories." *Greensboro News and Record.* July 27, 2008.

———. "Old mill prospered early in the 20th century." *Greensboro News & Record.* August 3, 2008.

"Oakdale Cotton Mills committed to community." *High Point Enterprise.* March 29, 1995.

Oakdale Cotton Mill Village. National Register of Historic Places Inventory-Nomination Form, 1975.

Ragsdale, J. S. to Hon. Thomas Settle, letter. Jamestown, NC: January 29, 1895, in W. L. Eury Appalachian Collection, Special Collections, Appalachian State University, Boone, NC.

Historical Organizations in Jamestown

Originally settled about 1760, Jamestown is one of the oldest communities in Guilford County. Several history-specific organizations are active here. Each plays its own part in preserving the town's history.

The Historic Jamestown Society was organized in the 1970s. It is located at the Richard Mendenhall Plantation, built in 1811; listed on the National Register of Historic Places; and operated as a museum. Its mission is to collect and preserve the history of Jamestown. For more information, see www.mendenhallplantation.com. Its location is 603 West Main Street, Jamestown, North Carolina.

The Old Jamestown School Association was organized in the 1980s to save and restore the old Jamestown School, built in 1915. The school building now houses the Jamestown Public Library. Its location is 200 West Main Street, Jamestown, North Carolina.

Jamestown Alumni Archives is also in the old Jamestown School, operated by the Jamestown Alumni Association. Its mission is to preserve the history of education in Guilford County. The Ragsdale Collection is here currently, but since it does not fall within the mission of this group, it is slated to be moved elsewhere. The North Carolina Echo Web site includes information about this organization in its directory.

In 2006, the authors initiated the Oakdale Mill Project to collect the histories of the mill, the village, and the people associated with them. The Historic Jamestown Society sponsored the project, and the primary result of that project is a DVD, *Oakdale Cotton Mills: Close-Knit Neighbors*, filmed by Mary Dalton and published by the Historic Jamestown Society.